MORE
TALES OF A GLOUCESTER BLOKE

MORE
The True Story of a Bloke
TALES OF A
GLOUCESTER BLOKE

Memoirs of Bill Lawrence

WILLIAM LAWRENCE
and
J.L.L ANDRUSZKIEWICZ

ISIS
LARGE PRINT
Oxford

MORE
TALES OF A
GLOUCESTER BLOKE

Memoirs of Bill Lawrence

WILLIAM LAWRENCE
and
JILL ANDRUSZKIEWICZ

ISIS
LARGE PRINT
Oxford

Copyright © William Lawrence and Jill Andruszkiewicz, 2006

First published in Great Britain 2006
by ISIS Publishing Ltd.

Published in Large Print 2006 by ISIS Publishing Ltd.,
7 Centremead, Osney Mead, Oxford OX2 0ES
by arrangement with
William Lawrence and Jill Andruszkiewicz

The moral right of the author has been asserted

British Library Cataloguing in Publication Data
Lawrence, William
     More tales of a Gloucester bloke. – Large print
     ed. – (Isis reminiscence series)
     1. Lawrence, William
     2. Blue collar workers – England – Gloucester
     – Biography
     3. World War, 1939–1945 – Personal narratives,
     British
     4. Large type books
     5. Gloucester (England) – Biography
     I. Title   II. Andruszkiewicz, Jill
     942.4'1082'092

ISBN 0–7531–9334–5 (hb)
ISBN 0–7531–9335–3 (pb)

Printed and bound in Great Britain by
T. J. International Ltd., Padstow, Cornwall

This book
is for our family with all our love.

We would like to thank Ted,
Hilda Klap and Laura Lopez
for all their help and encouragement.

CONTENTS

CONTENTS

CHAPTER
ONE

Home Again

The sight of my wife, Sally, and our daughter Jill running along the empty railway station platform to meet me was a memory that would remain with me forever. It had been three and a half years since we had last seen each other.

In the heat and dust of North Africa and Italy, where I had been during the war, there had been times when I wondered if I would ever see my family or Gloucester again, but here I was with my feet planted firmly on English soil once more, hugging my little girl with one arm and embracing Sally with the other, kissing her like there was no tomorrow. It felt good to be home.

To celebrate the occasion we took a taxi home that day, even though it was only a short walk from the L.M.S. railway station through the black alley — named after the locomotive clinker that covered the ground — to where we lived in Millbrook Street. Jill was delighted to travel home in such luxury since our usual form of transport had never gone beyond a bus or a bicycle, and then only if it was too far to walk. When we arrived at 130 Millbrook Street, there was a banner over the top of the front door welcoming me home and

1

several neighbours standing on their doorsteps, waving and calling out greetings.

Jill was the first out of the taxi, running into the house calling "Gong Gong, Gong Gong — Daddy's home!" I grabbed my luggage and we followed her in. Sally's father, Tom Jefferies, who I called Dad, was sitting in his large wooden chair positioned in the corner of the room next to a roaring fire when I entered. It was just as I remembered him. When he saw me he pulled himself up out of the chair and we greeted each other with watery eyes and much backslapping.

Jill always called him Gong Gong. We never knew why, but it caused much amusement over the years. Sometimes when she mentioned his name in company, a look of disbelief would spread across the listener's face, and when it was confirmed that Jill always called him that, curiosity would enter the equation as they tried to work out the mysterious Oriental connection — but there was none. The only thing remotely connected was a small ornamental brass gong that stood on the sideboard, but since Dad never chased her with it, as far as we were aware, we dismissed that idea. Besides, Jill showed no fear of it, in fact it was just the opposite since she would strike it at every opportunity, annoyingly so sometimes, to announce that dinner, breakfast, tea, or anything else that was going, was "being served". In the end we concluded it was because she hadn't managed to get her tongue around "Grandfather" when she first started to talk and ended up with "Gong Gong" instead, and the name stuck.

Soon we were all sitting round the table and Sally was pouring cups of hot tea from the pot that Dad had already brewed in anticipation of our arrival. There was so much to talk about we hardly knew where to start. The next thing Mrs. Campbell, our good friend and neighbour who also happened to be the landlady of the Windmill pub next door, was hanging over the six-foot high whitewashed wall which separated us from the pub with a bottle of beer in her hand, slightly greying hair still set close around her smiling face.

"Bill, Bill," she called out. I went into the scullery and opened the door into the backyard. " 'ave this one on me, Bill, and God bless you — welcome home!" I thanked her and reached up and took it. Then she was gone and I could see beyond to the upstairs club rooms where Sally and I had held our wedding reception. Memories flooded back — so much had happened since then — so much to catch up with.

I glanced up the yard and noticed that the long tin bath was still hanging in the same spot on the wall, next to the wooden meat safe. Ready for Friday nights, our usual bath night, when copious amounts of water would be heated and the bath would be brought into the scullery and placed on a coconut mat, supposedly to stop the coldness of the stone floor striking through to the bather. It didn't do much good, though. Besides, with four people to bathe, none of us had the luxury of just soaking. It was more like "Get in — soap all over — rinse off — NEXT!".

Then Dan Cove from the fish and chip shop opposite, who had nurtured Sally and my courtship by

3

lowering his shop lights when we kissed goodnight, was knocking on the front door and another cup of tea was poured. It seemed we never stopped talking for hours.

The house belonged to Mitchells and Butlers Brewery and Sally's father and mother had lived in it for years. Before the war Sally and I lived a bit further down Millbrook Street, but when her mother died suddenly after I had joined up, Dad suggested that Sally and Jill move in with him. It seemed the sensible thing to do at the time since we didn't know how long the war was going to last or what the outcome would be. He also officially changed the name of the tenant to Sally — "just in case," he said.

It was a very small house with two rooms downstairs and two bedrooms upstairs. A guide to the size of the rooms can be gauged by the fact that none of the rooms were big enough to hold an upright piano and open the doors at the same time, which Sally said was a great disappointment when she was growing up, since everybody seemed to have a piano in their parlour except her.

The scullery was attached to the back of the house, which opened into a small narrow yard containing an outside toilet, a coalhouse and a lean-to shed. Beyond the shed was a small garden crammed full with chrysanthemums, tomatoes, parsley, mint and two huge clumps of lavender. At the end of the short path was another small shed attached to a high wall belonging to the pub. A wooden fence separated us from our other neighbour and beyond that were other gardens with their jumble of fences, sheds and clotheslines, ending with the garden of Barnes's sweet shop which stood on the corner. A narrow alleyway by the side of it led to some dark grimy red brick houses set well back off the road. Rising above it all, about 200 yards away, was the Derby Road Senior School, a large, impressive, two-storey brick building next to a smaller infants' school. The buildings were completely surrounded by very tall black pointed iron railings, regularly punctuated by large round white stone columns with red dome tops.

The railings which had been around the small front garden of 130 hadn't faired so well. In fact they were non-existent now, having been ripped out and taken away, like hundreds more in the area, for the "War Effort". All that was left were the gaping holes. When I went away there had been a garden full of flowers and Dad would often use the front windowsill as a seat in the warmer weather and watch people go by while he smoked his Woodbines. Now it looked very different. Besides the missing railings, the ground was all rough and trampled on and that night I found the reason.

Sometime during my first evening home, I heard some noise outside the front door and went to investigate and found a pile of bicycles leaning against the front of the house.

"There's some bikes outside, Dad," I said. "Do you know who they belong to?"

"No, I don't," he said. "They're a bloody nuisance. It's some railway blokes stopping off for a pint next door after work, before going home. They're not from round here. If I catch 'em I tell 'em to clear off, but they're back again the next night! Said the house belonged to the Brewery anyway!"

"And we pay the rent!" said Sally.

"We'll soon fix their little game," I said, feeling suddenly angry. "Right, that will be my first job this week." I made this my priority and by the end of the week there was a fence around the garden again.

Amazingly the trespassers were upset with the new addition and said so when they saw me.

"That wasn't very clever," said one of them. "Now where am I going to put my bike?" So I told him!

The view from the back bedroom window stretched away beyond our bottom wall across a maze of backyard fences and sheds belonging to the people living round the corner from us, in Windmill Parade. In the distance, silhouetted against the sky, stood the tall chimneys of the Alfred Street Foundry.

Many people had taken to keeping chickens during the war because of the food rationing, and judging from the cacophony that woke me at the crack of dawn on my first morning home, there were many cockerels amongst them. Sally told me that whenever she collected a bucketful of vegetable peelings, she would send Jill with it, round to Mr. Ravenhill who lived in Windmill Parade. "As a 'thank you'," she said, "he would always go and check his chickens' nest boxes and if there was an egg to spare he would give it to her. I always told Jill not to expect an egg every time, so when she did get one — and it was still warm — it was something special".

6

The day after my return Sally, Jill and I took a walk to see my family. I was one of three children and had been born in a very poor area of Gloucester named Kingsholme, but commonly known as Clapham. My mother died of the Spanish Flu when I was aged six and a half. From that time until I married I had lived with my grandparents, except for a brief period when I returned to my father after he remarried, but it hadn't worked out.

My grandparents had a shop in Council Street, which was now run by a daughter, Aunt Else. At the time of my mother's death, my sister Lilian — who was only three and a half, was temporarily taken in by my father's sister Aunty Rose, and my younger brother, Baby Wally, who was only six months old, was looked after by Granny Newman, an old lady living nearby. They both later went back to live with my father.

His was the first house we visited. Things hadn't always been good between us with one thing and another, mostly, I felt, because of his indifference towards me earlier in my life. Nevertheless, I was pleased that he looked so well. We greeted each other warmly and he told us that Wally, who had been serving in the Merchant Navy, was home safe, as was Lilian's husband, Les Huggins, who had been in the Army. It was good news — I could see there was going to be a lot of catching up to do.

Next we saw Aunt Annie and Uncle George, who lived around the corner. I was very fond of both of them. They had been very good to me when I was growing up. Uncle George had often taken me fishing

7

or collecting snails when I was young. We were overjoyed to see each other again and Aunt Annie gave Jill another of her neatly ironed embroidered handkerchiefs. She seemed to have an endless supply because whenever Jill visited, she would always conjure one up from somewhere.

Finally we reached the shop. It was good to see my Grandfather again, still sitting in his usual high backed wooden chair, looking clean and smart as ever — he had always taken a pride in how he looked. My grandparents had been my guiding light in my younger years, especially m'Gran, who always had a story or a parable to suit every occasion, and although I can't remember her going to church regularly, she insisted that I went to Sunday School every week. Unfortunately she died when I was in my teens.

We all sat and talked for a while with Aunt Else darting backwards and forwards into the shop, which was in the front of the house, to serve customers. Word travelled fast down Clapham way and soon other neighbours and relatives were popping their heads in to say "hello". Sally and Jill had been regular visitors to Clapham during the war and sometimes Jill had gone with John and Jippy, Uncle Albert's two sons, out to his farm at Sandhurst, especially when an extra hand, even a small one, was needed during the harvesting of potatoes.

We all sat around reminiscing, swapping our experiences over the absent years.

"And we sorted out a few things while you were away, didn't we, Vi?" chuckled Aunt Else.

(Everyone except me called Sally Vi — short for Violet. It's a long story about a lovely girl who didn't like her name Violet and chose to tell her boyfriend at the time — me — that her name was Sally because she liked it better, and the name stuck.)

"What was that?" I asked, but Sally quickly put her finger to her lips behind Jill's back and mouthed "later".

That evening when Jill was in bed and Dad had gone next door to the Windmill for his usual pint, I asked her what all the secrecy was about.

"Well, it all started when I went looking for Jill one day. I knew she was playing somewhere near the allotments with some other kids and found her climbing the railings over the tunnel," she said.

"What! You mean the one by the side of the Foundry?"

Sally nodded. I remembered it well. The way to the allotments was through the tunnel which ran down besides the Foundry and under a very wide stretch of railway lines to emerge on the other side between fenced railway sidings, fields and allotments. It was wide enough for cyclists to pass each other but not enough for a car. Further on the path led over still more railway lines, via the Tea Bridge. Then there was a stile and eventually the path ended in Eastern Avenue. The tunnel was about twelve feet high and railings ran over the entrance to it, first to fence off the railway lines and secondly to protect any railway employee who happened along there on a dark night from an early

9

death. It was a long way to fall for anybody, let alone a child.

"What the hell was she doing up there?" I asked.

"Apparently one of the boys she was playing with had done it first and said Jill wouldn't be able to do it because she was a girl."

"So she had to prove she could!"

"Yes, something like that. You can imagine how I felt when I saw her slowly stepping across the top, holding on to the railings, sticking her feet into the spaces between the uprights — I nearly died. She had her back to me so she couldn't see me coming, but one of the other kids shouted to her and she stopped dead — right over the middle of the tunnel. There was nothing I could do but to tell her to carry on to the other side whilst I stood underneath, ready to catch her if she fell! Once she was safely down I really gave her a good scolding and made her promise that she would never do it again."

"So what happened?"

"Nothing at first and I thought that was the end of it until about a week later when I caught her at it again. She said somebody had dared her — so she had to do it."

"What did Dad say about all this?" I asked.

"I didn't tell him; he'd have gone up the wall and never come down if he knew! I realized something had to be done quickly before an accident happened. The next thing they would be daring each other to jump across the railway lines or something stupid like that — even though I had drummed it into her to keep off

10

railway property. She is full of energy and a bit of a tomboy. By the way things were going I knew she wouldn't be able to resist the challenge. I couldn't keep my eye on her all the time and I couldn't expect Dad to be doing the same; he was still working — so I went and saw Aunty Else and asked her advice about it."

"Why didn't you write and tell me about it?" I asked.

"There wasn't much point in telling you — you had enough things on your mind. Besides, it was something that had to be sorted out this end. Anyway, Aunt Else told me not to worry, she'd think of something and to send Jill down to see her the following weekend — so I did."

"Did she tell you what she was going to do?" I asked.

"No," said Sally. "Anyway, I waited to see what was going to happen and when Jill returned she was really quiet, not at all her usual self. I asked her if she'd had a nice time and she said she had, but the strange thing was that over the next week she wasn't at all keen on playing outside after school, not even in the street, let alone going anywhere near the allotments. I was starting to get concerned. After all, usually I had a job to keep her in the house and now it was just the opposite. In the end I nipped down to Aunt Else on my bike after I had finished work one morning, while Jill was at school, and asked her what had happened, telling her about Jill's unusual behaviour since her return.

" 'Well, that's good — it must be working,' she said and went on to tell me what she had done. Aunt Else told Jill that she'd had a visitor the week before. A

11

policeman had turned up at the shop, she said, asking if she knew any small dark haired girl with blue eyes, aged about seven or eight (*an obvious description of Jill*). She said she asked the policeman what it was all about and he told her that there had been a report of a girl fitting that description who had been seen climbing on railway property and she was in a lot of trouble."

I couldn't help laughing at Aunt Elsie's ingenuity.

Sally continued: "Aunt Else said that Jill went quite pale at that point, and she asked her, 'You don't know anybody who would have done anything so silly do you?' Jill just shook her head and Aunt Else said: 'I didn't think you would — I told him I didn't know anybody like that, but the policeman said they were still looking out for her and if anything turned up I was to tell him'."

"Did she do it again?" I asked.

Sally shook her head. "Wouldn't go anywhere near the tunnel on her own for ages afterwards. She'd only walk up with Dad or me if we went to pick some vegetables, and even then she'd run like blazes through the tunnel as quickly as possible and wait for us on the other side."

"Just in case *the policeman* spotted her," I said, and we laughed.

"That's right," said Sally, "it must have been at least a month before she would go up there on her own again. Aunt Else mentioned the visitor again, casually, on a couple of subsequent visits, just in case Jill was tempted again — but it did the trick."

CHAPTER TWO

The Thanksgiving Service

A couple of days after my return Sally and I thought we would take a leisurely walk into town and, on reaching the Cross, decided to walk further on down Westgate Street and visit Gloucester Cathedral. Sally said she had often gone there with Jill during the war to walk around inside it, through the cloisters, past the various chapels — and to say a prayer. We hadn't walked far before the Shire Hall, containing the Law Courts, came into view on the left hand side and memories came flooding back. I had worked as a telegraph boy when I was in my teens, and on one occasion had been on duty there. A woman named Mrs. Pace had been on trial, accused of murdering her husband by arsenic poisoning. It was my job to race off to the nearest Post Office with the latest news from Press Reporters sitting in the courtroom, each of them trying to get their stories out first.

We turned into College Street on the opposite side of the road and the Cathedral, with its magnificent tower, came into view. The air was frosty. Wintry sunshine highlighted its sculptured façade, casting shadows here and there. It was like another homecoming and suddenly it struck me how attached I was to the place. Not that I had visited the Cathedral every five minutes before I went away, but more that it had always been there in the background — somewhere — when I thought of home, even bragging about it to my mates if the subject of cathedrals came up.

How many had been greeted with the same sight and emotion over the years, I wondered? Due to the age of the structure, it wasn't hard to imagine there had been countless such experiences.

The building of the present Cathedral didn't commence until A.D.1089. Before that time there was the Abbey of St. Peter, which was founded by Osric as a Community of monks and nuns. King Henry III was crowned there and in 1450 many pilgrims visited the tomb of Edward II, believing it held mystic healing powers. They would stay at an Inn built especially for them, named the "New Inn", situated in Northgate Street. Practically next door to the Inn was a Lane called Oxebode Lane (pronounced Oxbody), and an old local nursery rhyme illustrates just how narrow it was.

> There's an ox lying dead at the end of the Lane,
> His head on the pathway, his feet in the drain.
> The lane is so narrow, his back is so wide,
> He got stuck in the road 'twixt a house on each
>   side.
> He couldn't go forward, he couldn't go back.

He was stuck just as tight as a nail in a crack
And the people all shouted, so tightly he fits
We must kill him and carve him and move him in
   bits.
So a butcher dispatched him and then had a sale
Of his ribs and his sirloin, his rump and his tail,
And the farmer he told me, I'll never again
Drive cattle to market down Oxebody lane.

Anon.

As early as A.D. 48 Roman soldiers were established at Kingsholme — my birthplace — most likely because of its proximity to the River Severn and the fact it was the lowest defendable crossing point. They believed it was a good place for them to commence their campaign to suppress the Welsh tribe in south Wales. It didn't work, though, because whenever there was a rugby match on at the Kingsholm Rugby Club and a Welsh side was playing, they'd all come back over the border in droves to cheer on their side. And whether they won the game or not, they'd always try and sing the opposition to death. Some time later Gloucester was born with the Roman name of Glevum. So much history surrounded us and we took it all for granted. It was all part of being a Gloucester Bloke and I couldn't imagine it any different.

We crossed College Green and to our left we could see St. Mary's Gateway, where Queen Mary I sat and watched Bishop Hooper, the Protestant Reformer, being burnt at the stake.

"Always makes me shudder when I think of what happened to Bishop Hooper," said Sally. "They were a bloodthirsty lot in those days, weren't they?"

I agreed.

"Sometimes, while you were overseas, I would take Jill to Bishop Hooper's Museum. We spent hours in there, especially if the weather was cold and we were looking for somewhere to go. We loved the place, the smell of it, all that old timber. Jill was as fascinated with the slanting floors as she was with the exhibits. I usually ended up sitting and talking to the assistant while she explored the place."

When we reached the main entrance to the cathedral we found it had been cordoned off and a policeman was on duty. A notice was posted on a stand a few paces in front of him:

A THANKSGIVING SERVICE
WILL BE HELD AT 3p.m. TODAY
FOR THE SAFE RETURN OF THE
MEN AND WOMEN
WHO HAVE SERVED THEIR COUNTRY
DURING THE WAR.

I checked my watch and found that it was ten minutes to three.

"What do you think?" I said, looking at Sally. She agreed that it seemed the right thing to do and we headed for the main entrance, though actually getting into the cathedral was not so easy as we thought. The policeman standing on duty, who had watched us while we read the notice and had heard our discussion, now asked us for our invitations and when we said we had none he refused our entry, saying it was by "invitation only".

"That's a good one!" I said.

"I'm sorry, sir," he said. "But that's the way it is. The Mayor and City Councillors and other leading members of the Gloucester Community are all inside — it's full."

I grabbed Sally's arm and turned away. "C'mon," I said, feeling disgruntled, but Sally was in no mood to take it lying down.

"And what about those men who've just got home — what about them? My husband's just got back after three and a half years overseas, serving his country like lots of others, and now he's not even allowed to attend a Thanksgiving Service. It don't make sense!"

I'd never seen Sally so fired up before and an old man who had been standing near the entrance came over.

"Is that right — you've just got back after all that time?" he asked me.

"Yes," I replied.

"Wait here!" he said. "Give me a couple of minutes and I'll be back."

So we stood and talked to the policeman, who turned out to be quietly sympathetic. Soon the old man returned and told us to follow him into the Cathedral. The policeman had been right when he said it was full — we couldn't see an empty seat anywhere; it was absolutely packed. I expected that we would be allowed to stand at the back, but instead we were led to the far side of the cathedral and then down towards the front. I'd forgotten how big the nave actually was inside, and how hollow everything sounded as the sound of our heels clinked on the stone floor, even though we tried to walk quietly.

We followed the old man past huge stone columns, reaching over thirty feet high, the side walls crammed with stone memorials. Large slabs marking ancient burials passed beneath our feet and still we moved even closer to the Altar. Then just as I began to wonder if we might be heading for a side chapel, or somewhere else of that nature, where we could still hear the service even if we couldn't see what was going on, we reached the front of the congregation. To our amazement we were shown two empty seats, which we could see had been added on to a row where some "Old Contemptibles" (old soldiers from the regular army in 1914) were already seated. It was an honour to be sitting next to them and gave added meaning to the service. Almost immediately the cathedral organ began to play, filling the air with its thunderous, rapturous music and the very moving service began. I have never forgotten it.

CHAPTER
THREE

Millbrook Street

When I had time to look around, it was clear that some people in the area had not faired so well. Bombs had been dropped on the corner of Twyver and Millbrook Street and several houses had received a direct hit. I stood looking across the bombsite one morning and was shocked to see the back fence of our old house, where we had been living before I joined up, on the edge of it. I was glad Sally and Jill had moved in with her father.

On the other side of the road was another bombed-out area in the shape of a triangle, formed by the black alley dividing into two separate paths, at right angles, before continuing on to join the street. One path followed a slight curve towards the upper part of Millbrook Street, whilst the other ran along the fenced-off Mill Brook to join the lower part. There was a factory on the other side of the Brook, where we took our radio batteries to be recharged.

The triangular area was large enough for one good-sized building and within a short time an Elim Pentecostal Church was built there. From then on, over several years, the building would vibrate every Sunday

19

as the overflowing congregation let forth with the sound of joyful, spirited hymns, telling everyone within hearing distance to "Praise the Lord! Praise the Lord!".

"Must 'ave a full 'ouse tonight!" would be a local comment on hearing the vocal strength. They certainly enjoyed themselves and I imagined that everyone would return home, afterwards, feeling completely exhausted and believing "a good time was 'ad by one an' all". I often wondered what the church was like inside, but never dared venture in. Nobody I knew seemed to know either. It was all a bit of a mystery.

Different to walking inside a church like St. Mark's or All Saints, or Gloucester Cathedral if I was nearby, where you could quietly go in any time and sit for a while if you felt like it. The Elim church wasn't like that. It appeared to be either locked up and empty or bursting at the seams. I have to admit I never went to check the closed doors. There didn't seem to be any opportunity for a bloke to take a quiet look around inside the place on his own. Nevertheless the neighbourhood certainly seemed livelier on Sundays after they moved in.

Later, Sally told me about when the bombs fell.

"Jill and me were down the air raid shelter at Derby Road School when it happened," she said. "Dad wasn't with us that time — he only came to the shelters once, the first time the sirens went. That was enough for him, he said. He wasn't going to be chased out of his own home again by anybody, he didn't care who or what they were, he was going to stay in his own bed, and refused to budge. So when we heard the bombs drop, and everything shook, we knew it was close by and people began to get a bit frightened. Everybody was hoping it wasn't their house, but we knew it had to be somebody's and from the sound of it, nearby. When the "all clear" went we all came out and looked around; it was still dark and we couldn't see much — no fire or anything like that. It wasn't until the next morning that we found out the bottom of Twyver Street had been hit.

"Jill and I raced home to see if our house was still there. It was a relief to see it still standing. Then when we tried to open the front door it was jammed. We could hear Dad on the other side doing his best, but in the end some passing railwaymen helped push the door in. There wasn't a door or window in the house which opened or closed properly after that night, and about a week later I was sat out cleaning our bedroom windows when the window got stuck on my lap, and I couldn't move it. (*The way Sally cleaned the sash windows was to push both of them up and then pull herself outside, with her back to the street, and sit on the windowsill. Then the windows were pulled down one at a time on to her lap for cleaning. Sally never seemed to notice how dangerous it was - both her and her mother had always done it that way - besides, who could afford to pay a window cleaner?*) Jill ran upstairs and tried to shift it with me but it was no good and in the end I had to call out to a man riding past on his bike, to come and help. Everybody said the bombers must have been after the railways and the gasometers."

Two of the huge fuel containers stood on the other side of the Horton Road railway crossing and would have done a lot of damage if they had been hit. I began to realize how lucky they had been.

"Then others," continued Sally, "said the bombs dropped on Gloucester were ones left over from the raids on Coventry and Birmingham and they just wanted to get rid of the things before they flew back to Germany."

That seemed to make more sense when we thought about it. Compared with the awful destruction of London and other major cities, Gloucester got off lightly — except for the poor people who got hit, of course. We all knew that normally when the enemy had *intended* bombing a place they'd made a good job of it, with ruins to prove it! Another story which circulated was that the cathedral was spared because the German pilots used it to direct them to their target elsewhere.

Millbrook Street was a different street to the normal kind. It wasn't straightforward like the normal streets where you could stand in the middle and see both ends. Rather it snaked itself up from Barton Street — the main local shopping area — to the wide railway crossing in Horton Road, and the adjoining big railway sheds. Anyone not familiar with the layout of the street automatically thought it finished on the last curve where Derby Road connected with it, and we were often mistaken for living in that road. Some outsiders even suggested we should apply to change the street name to make it easier for everybody, but the people along our stretch were quite indignant at the suggestion. We liked the way things were — being in Millbrook Street — and our exclusiveness. Compared with other streets in the vicinity, it was quite long. From one end to the other it was a ten minute walk and housed four pubs, one off licence, a fruit and veg shop, several small grocery, sweet and tobacco shops and one fish and chip shop which was directly opposite our house. So you could say that the locals' needs were well catered for. We always joked that we would never go hungry or thirsty with a pub next door and Dan Cove's fish and chip shop opposite. One of the small shops was on the corner of Windmill Parade and Millbrook Street, opposite the Windmill. Dan Cove's mother owned it. It was open all hours and she did a thriving business with the passing traffic to and from the railway yards, selling a little bit of everything, but mostly cigarettes and sweets. Mrs Cove senior was a small, round, dimpled, old lady with thinning white hair pulled back into a tiny bun at the back of her head. She had a very sharp business mind when it came to making money and never missed an opportunity. Whatever it was, if she could tie it up into a bundle and it fitted on the counter or in a corner on the floor, she'd have a price on it.

Opposite us, on the railway side of the fish and chip shop, lived Charlie Smith, the men's hairdresser. He carried on his hairdressing business in the converted front room of his house, a room with dark green walls and floors covered with shabby brown linoleum. Several wooden chairs, with reading material, stood against the wall. Over the fireplace, opposite the

23

barber's chair, was a large mirror. A central light hung on a long cord directly over the customer. Because the glass in the lower part of the window was frosted, there was no indication outside in the street of how many men might be waiting for a haircut or who was in the chair. And since it was the kind of establishment where men would be expected to "come and go" throughout the day, it was a good cover for his other business which took place in the back room - a lucrative betting shop.

In complete contrast to his sparsely furnished hairdressing room, his betting shop contained so much furniture, paintings and general clutter that there was hardly room to move. And when that side of his business was open Charlie sat behind a large table in the centre of it. Piles of racing papers and betting slips surrounded him, with a cash box sitting within easy reach. Again a light hung low in the centre of the room, illuminating all transactions. Money was everything to him and whenever I saw him sitting there he always reminded me of Scrooge.

The only time anyone in our house gambled was when the Grand National and the Derby horse races were run. On those occasions we all picked a horse — even Jill — and I would go and put the four bets on with Charlie, just for the fun of it. They were only small ones, something like a shilling each way.

"Want to throw yer money away, then?" he'd say, giving one of his rare laughs as he scooped the coins up. But if you won a race and went to collect your winnings, he was a different person altogether and would almost throw the winnings at you.

Charlie had a housekeeper named Lil Moyle, a small chatty little woman, who often popped over to our house for a cup of tea. She lived there with her two children, a son and daughter, and also worked for the local Co-operative driving a horse and cart, delivering milk in the early hours of the morning every day of the year (except Christmas Day, I think). Her daughter, Anne, was a friend of Jill's and sometimes, on a Sunday morning, Lil would take them both with her to deliver the milk as a treat — although it was against the Company policy to do so. To solve the problem she would arrange to meet the girls in a nearby street outside the depot. Jill thought it great fun, especially when she was momentarily allowed to hold the horse's reins in a quiet lane somewhere.

Anne's grandfather, Lil's father, lived around the corner in Millbrook Street opposite the County Arms and worked as a doorman at the Odeon Cinema. The two girls would go there on Saturday afternoon and buy two tickets for the cheapest seats, and then Anne's grandfather would smuggle them up into the balcony, where they would sit in the best seats in the front row.

Charlie Smith was already past middle age and suffered greatly from an ulcerated leg, which was always heavily bandaged. One day Lil ran over to our house, very distressed, asking if I could help — he had collapsed, she said, and she didn't know what to do. I ran back to the house with her. By now several neighbours, with some kind of primaeval intuition, had sensed there was something wrong and were gathering around the front door. We pushed our way between

25

them and ran up the passageway to the back room where Charlie was slumped awkwardly in his chair, looking paler than his usual shade of boiled suet pudding, his glasses askew on his face. I quickly tried to assess his condition, while the group at the front door did their own bit of speculation.

"What's wrong?"

"Dunno, 'e's collapsed — it's 'is leg, I think."

"What? You mean 'is leg's given way?"

"Wouldn't be surprised. 'E looked terrible the last time I saw 'im — white as a sheet 'e was."

"Not enough fresh air, that's 'is trouble. I'm a great believer in fresh air."

I recognized the voice of a woman who spent most of her day talking on her doorstep so I suppose she was speaking from experience. I loosened the clothing round his neck, but didn't know what I could do to help.

"Somebody better fetch the doctor," I said and Lil passed on my instructions down the hallway.

"Which one?" a woman's voice asked.

"The one next to the chemist in Barton Street," yelled Lil.

The instruction was echoed a couple of times amongst the women at the front door, then men's voices were heard, followed by a clatter of bicycles.

"Shouldn't be long — our Cyril's gone!" someone shouted.

I hoped Cyril wouldn't be long because the old man was looking worse by the minute.

"Could you get 'im upstairs to 'is bed for me?" Lil asked anxiously.

It was a big "ask". I was strong, but he was a big bloke and I wasn't sure if I could manage it.

"I'll try," I replied, putting his glasses safely on the mantelpiece. Lil quickly cleared a pathway to the door as I took a deep breath and heaved him up into a fireman's lift. Lil led the way, but carrying him up the narrow flight of stairs was no easy matter and before I was even a quarter of the way up I realized it was too much for me.

"I'm not going to make it — I can't 'old 'im — 'e's too 'eavy — 'e's pushing me back," I gasped, trying to hang on to the banister. Charlie and me were about to do a tumbling act back down the stairs, along the passage and into the bystanders with nothing to stop us. I could just see the headlines in the newspaper:

GOOD SAMARITAN BOWLS NEIGHBOURS OVER.

Before that could happen, however, one of the women standing at the front door, heard what I'd said and cried out: " 'ang on — we'll give yer a 'and," and the next thing there were at least three of them leaning into my back, holding me steady. Once I was balanced again, they pushed me hard from behind with such eagerness that if I had changed my mind and wanted to go backwards, they wouldn't have let me. Onwards and upwards they pushed and I remember thinking it was a pity that women didn't play rugby. This lot would have

27

been perfect in a scrum. It was a good job the fish and chip shop wasn't open next door, or we might have ended up with a whole team. Eventually we got to the top of the stairs and Lil guided me to his room in the front of the house, where I laid him on the large double bed. The members of the scrum stood in the doorway looking down at him.

"Poor bugger," said one, not missing a chance to do a quick scan of the bedroom to check the wallpaper, curtains and floor coverings.

"You looked after him well, Lil," said another, as if the poor bloke had already died.

"Probably wouldn't 'ave lasted as long as 'e did, without your 'elp," said another, and the room fell silent as we all stood and looked at him, now deathly white and very still. Then as if to let everybody know he was still in the land of the living he stirred slightly and the women jumped.

"We'll go and 'ave a look if the doctor's coming," someone said and they all quickly disappeared back down the stairs.

As it turned out I shouldn't have responded to Lil's request to take Charlie upstairs, but should have left him in his chair where he fell, because when the doctor came he called for an ambulance and the old man had to be brought all the way back down the stairs again. He ended up in hospital for a while.

Charlie Smith had a grown-up son who would visit him regularly. We always knew when he was around because there would be a magnificent gleaming car standing outside his house. I can't remember exactly what make it was, but it was something like a Bentley or Rolls Royce, and very grand. It was not the sort of car usually seen around Millbrook Street, and when it was parked outside Mr. Smith's house, a person might easily believe Royalty was visiting him.

On the other side of the fish and chip shop lived Mr and Mrs Kingston. They were both middle-aged and slightly overweight. When I think of them the description "round" comes to mind, Mr. Kingston more so than his wife. He was an Inspector on the railway and his whole life ran according to the railway timetable. Every time he heard a train go through the crossing — and we lived close enough to hear them all — it was commented upon, even in the midst of any conversation he might have been having at the time.

"I've got some good beans showing up in the back garden," he might say (*sound of engine going over crossing — pulls out silver pocket watch from his waistcoat and checks time*). "The Birmingham train's three minutes late — and the tomatoes don't look too bad either."

Mrs. Kingston, although "round" like her husband, was softer, plump and cuddly. She had a fair complexion and always looked freshly turned out. Sometimes she would drop in for a cup of tea and a chat when she had a spare moment and if there was a piece of cake going she would have a taste of that too. She was the neatest and daintiest eater I had ever seen, and would chase the last crumb around her plate with her thumb and forefinger until the plate was spotlessly

29

clean before handing it back. They had a daughter, Elsie, a lovely looking girl with a shock of curly auburn hair. Elsie and her friend were very keen cyclists and were members of a local cycling club. A quick run to Worcester, or any other place of equal distance, was nothing to them. She married an American serviceman during the war, named Levi, and went to live in the United States.

Several years later she came home for a holiday with her two young sons. They were very handsome boys and were always looking for ways to use up their energy. One day they found the ideal situation when Charlie Smith's son was visiting his father and left his big, beautiful car standing outside the house. Sally and I were sitting in our front room at the time, and saw it all.

Elsie's sons, not being familiar with the conditioned local response of "awe" in the presence of such automobile splendour, or the saying "don't touch what don't belong to yer!", could only see a big shiny climbing frame standing outside in the street just waiting for them to explore, and the next moment they were doing just that. Screeches of delight could be heard as they repeatedly clambered up on to the roof of the car and slid down the front windscreen and off the bonnet on to the road — twanging the windscreen wipers on the way.

We were in fits of laughter watching them, imagining what the car's owner would do if he caught them. Then, suddenly realizing that we should stop them before they either hurt themselves or were discovered, since the owner wouldn't be far away, we raced to the front door; however, Mrs Kingston and Elsie had beaten us to it and were already dragging them indoors, out of sight. Seconds later Mr. Smith's son was at his father's doorway, standing on the step, looking up and down the street, suspicious when he found it empty. He stepped down on to the pavement and looked at his car, then walked around it — then walked around it again. After a minute or two he went back into the house and shortly afterwards he left.

We often laughed, not unkindly, at opening gambits for a conversation used by some locals as they stood on their doorsteps for their daily airing, One old lady in particular always started with "Tent it awful?"-*isn't it awful?* — while other favourites were " 'eard the latest?" and " 'oodavberleeved it!" . We would always stop and have a quick chat. It was all part of being neighbourly. Later, at home, I might say " 'Tent it awful' said . . ." and everybody knew who I meant. They also recognized "The News of the World", who loved anything scandalous and was eager to pass on any gossip. Needless to say we avoided that person whenever possible.

Sometimes we adopted the various "sayings" ourselves, just for the fun of it. Like the time during the war when Sally and Jill went with Mrs. Kingston on a day trip to the Cheddar Gorge and on the way home they saw the house where Mrs. Kingston's sister lived way off in the distance but they couldn't stop. Smoke could be seen coming from the chimney.

"Oh, look — 'er's 'ome," Mrs. Kingston suddenly exclaimed, in her native Welsh lilt, pointing to her sister's house in the distance. "Our Blodwyn's got 'er fye-ah going."

It struck Sally and Jill as a phrase worth remembering — and remember it they did. Afterwards, whenever they saw smoke coming from a chimney belonging to someone they knew, they'd say "Oh look — 'er's 'ome — Aunt Else's got 'er fye-ah going" or "Oh look — 'e's 'ome — Gong Gong's got 'is fye-ah going".

Another family saying came about when they visited a relation named Aunty Kate who lived down the bottom part of Millbrook Street, near Barton Street. When they had visited her and she cut a piece of cake for them to eat, it was always so wafer thin that it had to be supported to get it on to the plate. After that if anyone in the family wasn't feeling very hungry when offered some cake at home, they'd say, "just an Aunty Kate's slice'll do". We had to stop using the expression later, though, after Aunty Kate visited us one day and Sally accidentally asked her if she wanted an ordinary slice or an "Aunty Kate's slice" and had to spend five minutes talking her way out of it.

Further down Millbrook Street, next to the Allington Hall, lived Freddie Burroughs, the local milkman. He wasn't a very big fellow and would have made an excellent jockey. He delivered the milk in all kinds of weather, on his bicycle. It had an attached trolley for the large milk churns to sit on. People left their covered jugs outside their front doors, often on a ledge or windowsill, and he ladled the milk into them.

Next to Freddie Burroughs lived Mr and Mrs. Finch. They had two daughters, Muriel and Mary. Muriel, the eldest, was married and lived at Weymouth, whilst Mary, who was somewhere in her twenties, was still single. She was a friend of Sally's and would pop over to the house at least one evening a week to fill her in on her latest romance. A bit like a soapy romance before the advent of television.

Opposite the Finches lived Mr. And Mrs. Barnes. Mr. Barnes was a keen fisherman and when the elvers were running in the Severn he would be there with his fellow fishermen after a catch. We always knew when he had been successful because the next morning a large clean white enamel bowl full of the wriggling baby eels would be placed on a chair on the pavement outside their house for locals to buy them, knowing they were really fresh. Sally and I loved them fried with bacon. Jill wouldn't go near them. First because they wriggled, second because they were transparent — you could see their minute heart beating inside — and thirdly, when they were cooked they turned white and their eyes were like two black dots on the end of a piece of string. She said she didn't like all those black eyes looking at her.

Next to the Barneses was a double-fronted house with a small walled forecourt. It was the biggest house in the area and much grander than the rest. The Bell family lived there and the person people knew best was "Peg", a woman who always had her finger on the pulse of Millbrook Street happenings and was there to offer help in times of need.

Peg's neighbour was the County Arms, a pub run by Mr and Mrs. Jones who had a very large family. I can't remember how many children they had, but there were a lot of them and they all seemed happy. Jill liked playing with the ones about her age and could often be found playing "statues" or similar games in the forecourt of the pub outside opening times.

Jill was asked if she would like to stay for lunch one day, and she raced home and begged us to agree.

"We all sat on wooden benches on each side of a big table," she said later, "which was ever so long — the room was really big as well — and Mrs. Jones put these enormous plates of bread and jam on the table and everybody just dived in."

"Was it nice?" Sally asked.

"I never got any."

We had to laugh at the last bit because we had always taught Jill to be polite and wait to be offered food when visiting other peoples homes, but could imagine when there were so many of them sitting down for a meal, such niceties would be forgotten. It was probably "he who grabs first gets fed". The Jones kids always looked well, though, so their survival instincts must have been good.

"Anyway," said Jill with a smile, "Mrs. Jones went and cut a piece specially for me." So it all ended well.

Meal times at our house were a lot different. One leaf of our dropped-leaf table would be put up for the meal and put down again afterwards. If we left it up there wasn't enough room to move about, and if we put up both leaves of the table, maybe for extra special occasions, such as Christmas or when we had visitors, only thin people could sit on the ends because they had to slip sideways into their seats. There was no room to pull chairs out. The only other time that both leaves were put up was when we had a game of table tennis. It was a very scaled down version of the proper game. The players squeezed in behind the ends of the table with their backs literally to the wall. Nevertheless it was a lot of fun because it ended up more like a game of squash with the ball hitting the walls and ceiling of the small room as the players tried to keep it in play.

All the children played in the streets. They were their playground, just like they had been mine when I was a child, although Clapham was more fortunate than Millbrook Street in that respect, because we had the "Rec" — a large recreation area with well-worn swings, a weathered roundabout and enough grass to kick a ball around, just around the corner from Council Street. The closest place for Millbrook Street children was the Gloucester Park, which was too far away. So the local streets became a large playground and if they were lucky, in winter, they could get a good long icy slide going down past the County Arms — if the old ladies didn't muck it up for them, by sprinkling salt on it when they weren't looking. At other times the street was an ideal place for roller-skating. There were hardly any cars on the road at that time, only essential vehicles like a doctor's, so it was comparatively safe.

A boy named Gordon Parsons, who lived around the corner in Windmill Parade, had a pair of roller skates and was very skilled on them, jumping, spinning and skating backwards. The locals would stop and watch him going through his routine. He would practice on an area where the street widened, between the Derby Road School and the Allington Hall, at the junction of Derby Road and Millbrook Street. Whenever he was there we knew where to find Jill, watching his every move. Needless to say she wanted a pair of skates, too, so Sally and I bought her some for Christmas. Within a short time, she was racing up and down the street, outside our house, jumping the manholes and collecting a few bumps and grazes on the way.

Some people thought that girls shouldn't be doing such things and frowned on the idea. Such was a railwayman who was quietly cycling home from work one day, completely lost in his own thoughts. Sally was sweeping the front doorstep and pavement at the time whilst Jill was practising her skating up and down the street, showing her mother her latest moves. She had just jumped one manhole — and was no doubt gaining speed for another jump, further along — when she whizzed past the man and frightened the daylights out of him. He wobbled about a bit and came to a stop, close to where Sally was sweeping the front of the house with her brush, not realizing that she was Jill's mother.

"Makes yer wonder what some mothers are like, don't it?" he said with disgust. "Letting ther daughters on the streets like that! 'Er nearly 'ad me off me bike racing past me like that!!"

Sally had missed the near collision and didn't know who he was referring to for a minute until he pointed at Jill in the distance, who by now had come to a stop near the closed Railway Crossing gates.

"Yes," said Sally, quickly, carrying on with the sweeping to hide her embarrassment and hoping he would go away. But he wouldn't be put off. He wanted to moan some more about "irresponsible mothers" and continued to do so. Meanwhile Jill, having turned around when she got to the closed gates at the railway crossing, saw both of them looking at her and thought she was needed and quickly skated back.

"Did you want something, Mum?" she asked.

"No, it's all right, love, you go and skate," Sally replied, at which point she stopped sweeping and proudly watched her skate away for good measure.

The railway man was so taken aback and indignant that he jumped back on his bike and rode off briskly down Derby Road without saying another word. And every time he passed the house after that, to and from work, he always looked determinedly ahead, not risking eye contact with anybody from our house. In fact it became a bit of a joke as to who could spot him first so that we could sweep the front and watch him ride past.

I hadn't been home long when I noticed the local kids clanking round on tin can stilts and naturally Jill wanted some as well, but I wasn't keen on the tin ones and decided to make her some proper wooden stilts instead. It had been a long time since I had been able to make something for her and I entered into the job with enthusiasm. Sally despaired when she saw them.

"There's me trying to make a young lady out of her and you're making her stilts!" But I enjoyed making them, and besides, it had been years since I'd used them myself, and I had to show Jill how they worked — didn't I? And there was that beautiful wide pavement outside the Derby Road School, where the kids played hopscotch, just asking for a pair.

In the end, even Sally couldn't resist it and had to have a go on them, much to everyone's amusement. And she wondered where Jill's adventurous spirit came from!

CHAPTER
FOUR

A New Job

At last my demob leave was coming to an end and I knew I would have to find a job soon. Most of my work before the war had been labouring, and although things had gradually improved as I worked my way up with the Gloucester Electricity Company, including taking on more responsibilities prior to my departure, I'd had enough of digging ditches and hoped that on my return from hostilities I would be skilled enough in some other trade to leave that daily exercise behind. The only time I wanted to pick up a spade in future was in the vegetable garden.

With my future in mind I chose the trade of cook when I enlisted in the Royal Air Force. There were always advertisements for cooks in the newspaper and if I was really good I might reach the heights of being a chef, although I soon learned that our training never reached that level. Our job was to cook good hearty healthy food to keep the airmen flying. Some, like my friend Jim Powell, had skills for higher things. He was very good with cakes and pastries, especially the decorating, and was soon nabbed by the Officers' Mess. Later, when I had learned all there was about basic cooking, reached the rank of corporal and was in charge of a group of men, it seemed my post-war dreams might at last be realised. At last I might obtain a position in the catering industry when I returned home instead of labouring again. All my hopes were dashed, however, when my hands broke out in dermatitis shortly before I was demobbed, putting an end to the whole idea. It looked like digging ditches for the Gloucester Electricity Company was going to be a reality again.

Not that they were a bad business to work for. On the contrary, they were extremely good. It was just the type of work I was fed up with. When I left to join up they even told me that they would keep my job open for me while I was away. And for the whole time I was enlisted, they voluntarily made up the monetary difference between my R.A.F. wages and the wages they had been paying me before the war. Sally went to their office once a week to collect the money. So in a way I felt obligated to return, but as the time drew nearer it didn't appeal to me one bit. There had to be something else, I thought.

Then, one morning as I was walking along George Street, fate took a hand when I bumped into an old friend, Mark Panter. We greeted each other warmly.

"I've just got m'self a job as a Security Policeman working for the Royal Air Force at Quedgely, out on the Bristol Road," he said. "It's bloody smashing."

"Lucky bugger!" I said.

Then he threw me a lifeline. "There's a job for you as well, if you want it. They're looking for ex-servicemen, especially from the R.A.F."

I couldn't believe it. It all sounded too good to be true and very exciting, a lot more interesting than digging ditches and laying cables. If I managed to get a job as a Security Policeman, all my prayers would be answered. Mark quickly gave me all the necessary contact information and I raced back home, grabbed my bike, and rode the five miles or so to the Camp. Within a couple of hours I had secured myself a job as a Security Policeman. I felt exhilarated. Wait till I tell Sally, I thought.

On the way back to Gloucester I decided to do the right thing and call into the Electricity Office and advise them that I would not be returning, but when I entered the reception area and asked to speak to the manager and gave my name, the receptionist gave me a big smile and said: "I'll just let the manager know you're here — he's been expecting you."

Expecting me? I hadn't made any appointment. Suddenly I felt uncomfortable.

The receptionist returned almost immediately.

"Go on in, Mr. Lawrence," she said leaving the door open for me to enter.

"Welcome back, William," the Manager said, reaching over and shaking my hand vigorously. He hadn't aged much since I last saw him. "It's good to see you after all this time. By the way, what part of the world did you end up in after all?" I told him and we chatted for a while before he asked: "Well, William, I'm really glad you're back — when do you want to start?"

I was taken aback by his keenness. It had been five years since I had joined up and to be welcomed back in such a way was totally unexpected.

"Well, it's like this," I said, suddenly feeling uncomfortable, "I've got another job," and went on to tell him about it as quickly as possible. He was obviously disappointed, surprisingly so, much more than I had anticipated; however, he shook my hand and wished me well in my new position and I made a hasty retreat.

When Sally learned about my new job she wasn't happy at all. Quite the contrary — she was very angry.

"How could you do such a thing after all they've done for us?" she said.

She was right, of course. How could I have done it? I realized I hadn't been fair to the Company. The least I could have done was to go back there, even if it was only for a short time and hope that a security job surfaced again later. But whether I would have been successful at a later date is another thing when they saw my last job was digging ditches. Besides, when Mark Panter told me about the job I wanted to see if I could get it then — not later — and being a Security Policeman sounded like a step in the right direction to me.

So here I was with a brand new job and everybody around me thinking I had done the wrong thing. I would soon find out if I had.

CHAPTER FIVE

Starting Work at Quedgeley

There was a pleasant nip in the air as I rode out to commence my new job at Quedgeley. A bus went that way, but the journey would have taken twice as long by the time I had walked into town to catch it. In the end my bike was the best option for me. Besides, Sally and I were trying to save and it would have cost too much. The cycle ride was both invigorating and enjoyable and I looked forward to taking the same journey every day. It made a change from the weather I had experienced over the previous couple of years; sweltering heat under canvas in North Africa, especially when the hot and dusty sirocco arrived in the spring making life unbearable. And that was before we started cooking.

I remember lying on my bed, trying to recall what it was like not to sweat. I would close my eyes and dream of cycling in the Gloucester countryside in the spring, or perhaps simply walking along Council Street or down Millbrook Street or anywhere. I didn't care where, providing it was in England and I was cool again. Just to see my fog-like breath in the frosty air. To look up at the millions of stars in a clear night sky and see a halo round the moon. To hear the crackle of frozen puddles beneath my feet.

Consequently, the possibility of inclement weather on my daily ride was greeted with relish. But, as usual where memories are concerned, I had only remembered the sentimental "chocolate box" scenes and not the freezing rain, sleet, snow, icy roads and winds that wanted to blow me all the way to Bristol. Whatever the weather I cycled through it. "It's what you wanted," I reminded myself as sleet beat down on my waterproof clothes and collected inside my scarf and collar. "And now you've got it!" came the reply. One consolation was that I must have been the fittest bloke in Gloucester by the time spring arrived.

The day I started my new job I was assigned to a small office at the entrance to the main Administration Building. There were about three or four other areas in the whole place besides the Admin., each having their own teams of men. Mark Panter was assigned to one of the others. Nothing seemed to happen much during my first week except a lot of sitting around in our office with occasional checks on things along the main corridors to make sure the police presence was noted. I found it very dull and not at all what I had expected it to be.

The police worked three shifts around the clock and it wasn't until I did my first night shift, when it was part of the job to leave the main office and patrol further afield, looking in all the nooks and crannies, including the empty offices, that things became a little more interesting. My companion for the first night was a policeman in his late thirties, named Ken. He was a pale-skinned bloke with dark hair already showing a sprinkling of white around his temples.

"Was that you I saw riding yer bike to work tonight?"

"Yes," I said.

"That's a mug's game — riding yer bike all the way out 'ere when there's a bus practically to the doorstep. Wouldn't catch me doing that!" Judging from his expanding waistline I believed him.

He had been working there for quite a while and was very keen to familiarize me with the perks of the job, pointing out various aspects, which he thought might interest me.

"You should see what these typists keep in their drawers!" he laughed, going to a desk and pulling a drawer open. He rifled through it for a moment before moving on to another.

"I didn't think we were supposed to look in there — that's private, isn't it?" I said, baulking at the idea. Looking at other people's personal items didn't interest me.

"That's what they say," he said. "But it's good for a laugh. You don't want to take any notice of everything you're told 'ere. Anyway, who's to know?" And he pulled open another drawer, picked up a bag of sweets and offered them to me.

"No, thanks," I said.

"Please yerself. This girl's always got a bagful." He poked about inside the bag deciding which one to pick. "Mmm — caramels — my favourite." When he found the one he liked, he dropped the bag back into the drawer and slammed it shut. Then he unwrapped the sweet and popped it into his mouth. "Thanks, love," he said to the typist's vacant chair before ceremoniously flicking the wrapper into a waste paper basket standing nearby.

He moved on to further pickings, opening a couple more drawers here and there as we went, taking a pencil from one and even stopping to read a letter from a third.

"Poor bugger," he commented after reading the first page and already turning to the second. "'er's 'aving trouble with 'er boyfriend. Looks like 'e lives in Swindon — well, that's what the address said on the top of the letter. Not much of a romance in that, is it — 'er being 'ere and 'im being all that way away?"

He placed the letter back in the envelope and returned it to the drawer.

As an afterthought he said, "I'd be surprised if 'e's not playing 'home and away'. Reckon 'er's better off without 'im."

There seemed no end to his curiosity, and just as I was wondering what kind of louse I had been lumbered with, he looked into yet another drawer in one of the larger offices and got what he deserved.

"What a bloody cheek!" he said.

I looked over his shoulder to see what the fuss was about. Inside the drawer was a large notice printed out in black ink:

HANDS OFF, NOSEY PARKER!

PUT EVERYTHING BACK
WHERE YOU FOUND IT!

Sometimes police dogs were delivered to us on night shifts, to help with the patrols. We were familiarised with the various directions to give the dogs and their responses, and then they were introduced to us and handed over. I had always imagined that the dogs remained only with their recognised handlers, but not in this case. With the few learned instructions my dog and I got on very well and the job didn't seem half so bad on those nights. I remember once, walking along a dimly lit path around the outside of the block. It was a moonless night and I had half finished the patrol, when the dog suddenly stopped, looked and pointed its nose into a particularly dark area.

"C'mon," I said, trying to pull it forward, thinking that it just wanted to dawdle — but there was no budging the animal. So I shone my torch in the direction the dog was pointing and to my surprise found another policeman, who I recognised from one of the other areas, with his girlfriend in the long grass.

It was obvious nothing got past that dog.

About three months after starting the job I bumped into a bloke who I knew worked in the office at the Electricity Co. and he asked how I was getting on with my new job.

"Not bad," I said, not wanting him to know how disappointed I really was.

"You know," he said, "they planned on offering you the foreman's job when you returned to work for them after the war. The Boss was really disappointed when you said you weren't coming back."

"What?" I said — I could hardly believe it.

"Oh, yes," continued my friend. "They ended up giving it to somebody who didn't know half as much about the job as you do."

I tried not to look too sick. If only I had known, how different things would have turned out. For a foreman's job I'd have willingly stayed with the Company.

"Anyway, that's life, I suppose. As long as you're happy where you are, that's the main thing."

If only, I thought.

There was a large warehouse on the Quedgeley site containing stacks of uniforms, which was guarded by another team of Security Policemen. We soon learned, on the grapevine, that some of the guards in charge of it had taken literally the quote "God 'elps them that 'elps themselves", instead of heeding the warning "sticky fingers have a sticky end". They all ended up in court charged with stealing, where they were found guilty and sent to prison.

After that, the Administration decided the best plan to combat any future crime was to regularly rotate the police around the different areas, which didn't make me very happy. I still had several shirts left over from my R.A.F. uniform, and wore them regularly to work. The last thing I wanted was to be accused of stealing from the store. So when shifts came into place and I was told to report to the Warehouse for duty, I refused. I told them my reasons and said if they insisted, I was leaving. They said all the Security Police had to rotate without exceptions — and that I couldn't leave without giving notice.

"All right," I said, "I'm giving a week's notice, now, but I'm still not working in that place." And I didn't. They let me stay where I was for the week and at the end I left. I learned later that Mark Panter had left the job after only three weeks — he hadn't liked it either.

Strangely enough, years later I was to become a Security Policeman again and that time I enjoyed it.

CHAPTER
SIX

Home Made Wine

Sally's father made wine. Not a lot of it, and the drop he did make was only shared with the chosen few who could keep their lips sealed. To brew homemade wine in a house owned by the brewery, and next door to one of its pubs, was not a good thing to do and most likely would have caused eruptions amongst the upper echelons of the Hops Industry if it was known. We had a feeling that Mrs. Campbell suspected the clandestine activity after a few passing comments of a cautionary nature but she never actually asked and we never spoke about it. If Dad sat out in the small backyard on a summer evening with a couple of his mates, enjoying a glass, he was always on the lookout in case she might pop her head over the wall. As a caution he would put a bottle of beer in the middle of the table and keep the wine beneath it.

The wine was brewed in the shed at the bottom of the garden and was made from either elderberry, parsnip or potato, depending on the fruit or vegetable in season, and whatever took his fancy at the time. Friends would often collect berries and deliver a basketful to him in the hope that sooner or later they would be invited in to taste the resulting brew. Whatever the ingredient, however, it was reputed to be a "good drop" by those who tasted it. I never tasted it myself. Although I had been offered some on numerous occasions, I preferred beer.

"I bet he knows exactly how much there is in them bottles down to the last drop," I commented to Sally one day, after seeing him disappear once more into the shed. He had disappeared in there with a basketful of parsnips a couple of days earlier, so we knew there was a new vintage brewing.

"He probably does," laughed Sally. "He knows we wouldn't touch it, but there was an incident, before we met, when I was still at school, which taught him to keep his eye on it."

"What was that, then?" I asked, full of curiosity.

"Well," said Sally, "it all started when Dad suspected that somebody was taking his wine. He knew that neither Mam nor me were guilty and all his suspicions fell on a Mrs. Bateman, who lived next door at the time. She was a big middle-aged woman with a grown-up family and always seemed to be under the influence. We all suspected that she was an alcoholic so she was the chief suspect. Of course, suspecting someone and actually catching them at it are two different things, but Dad was determined to get to the bottom of it.

"Once he had double-checked that the levels were dropping and somebody was definitely pilfering the stuff, he set about catching them. He started by turning his chair around in the living room to face the window so that he had a clear view straight up the garden path to the shed, and when he wasn't at work he would sit there and watch. This proved to be useless because he never saw anything suspicious, yet when he checked the levels of the wine it was clear that the thief was still at it. The only conclusion was that the pilfering was done when both he and Mam were out of the house at the same time, most likely whilst he was at work and Mam out shopping. He doubted if it was done after dark because he guessed that Mrs. Bateman would only do it when nobody else was at home, and in the evening there were always members of her family around.

"Dad realized that she must have been watching for them to leave the house. She could clearly see our front gate from her front room window and once she saw them both leave she knew she could help herself at leisure. So on his next day off, he sent Mam off shopping in Barton Street for an hour, while he dressed up in his normal work clothes and left the house, as if to go to work. He walked through the gate, turned right and walked past the Windmill as usual, but instead of going on to the railways, he nipped round the corner into Windmill Parade, where he waited. After a couple of minutes he returned to the house. It was just enough time for Mrs. Bateman to climb through the broken fence at the bottom of the garden, fill her small jug with Dad's wine — and be caught red-handed!

"By all accounts Dad really gave her a good telling off and she was so overcome by the shame of it all that she pleaded with him not to tell her husband. But Dad was so angry that he went ahead and told Mr.

Bateman, anyway. He told him to make sure he kept his wife over their own side of the fence in future.

"Little did he know that the man would react in the way he did, because that night there was a terrible row next door — we could hear it going on through the walls. He was calling her everything under the sun and she was screaming — it was terrible. You'd have thought there was a murder going on, and it was no good racing down to Hopewell Street Police Station to fetch a policeman, because we knew that they wouldn't interfere in a "domestic". You know how Mam used to wring her hands when she got anxious?"

I nodded; it was a thing I always remembered.

"Well, that night I thought she was going to wring her hands right off her arms."

"What happened to Mrs. Bateman?"

"We never saw her for about a week after that. Mam was getting worried about her, although we knew she was about somewhere because we'd hear her voice now and then. Besides, the washing was on the line — but nobody actually saw her.

"Then at the end of the week we found out why, when she ventured out of the house for the first time. Both her eyes had been blackened. She could only just see through two slits when we saw her, so the poor thing must have been blind for most of the previous week. Mam was furious with Dad over it. He said he regretted having said anything; he hadn't realized his neighbour would act so violently."

" 'I thought 'e'd give 'er a good telling off, not a bloody good 'iding,' Dad said. 'All I wanted was for 'im

53

to keep 'is wife out of our garden — and out of my drink!' Dad and Mam might have had their scraps but it was never more than heated words. It must be terrible to be in a family where that goes on."

"It is," I said, remembering when I was a child and seeing my father hit my stepmother, and the fear that consumed me and my younger sister Lilian at the time. I would never forget it.

"We'd always got on all right with the Batemans before," said Sally. "But after that things were never the same between the two families and it wasn't long before they moved out."

Another story concerning Dad's homemade wine and the potency of it was when I was visiting Sally at her home one evening when we were courting. Earlier the same day her father's face had collided with the side of a railway wagon resulting in a broken nose, so he was off sick and feeling pretty sorry for himself. When I arrived that evening and Sally opened the front door to me I was greeted by a strong smell of cigarette smoke, and when I entered the living room Sally's mother was busy trying to open a window to clear it.

" 'ello, Bill," she said. "Come and sit down if you can see where the chair is. 'e 'asn't stopped smoking since 'e's been 'ome." She rolled her eyes heavenwards.

"I keep telling you — it's bloody painful," Sally's father said.

I sat down and looked across at him sat in his chair by the side of the fireplace. A huge dressing covered his nose. I could just see his puffy bloodshot eyes peering over the top of it. Deep pink purple bruising was already showing and it was clear they would both be black by the morning. To add insult to his injury, his grey eyebrows and splendid moustache, which he had taken quite a pride in, were now reduced to a singed gingery frizzle.

"'ow's it going, then?" I asked, trying to make conversation. It seemed a stupid question when I already knew the answer.

"Bloody terrible," he said, stubbing his cigarette out into a full ashtray sitting at arm's length. Sally's Mam took it out, emptied it, and returned with a clean one, making small talk about the weather, while we all eyed him cautiously. You couldn't help feeling sorry for him as he gently rested his head against the back of the chair. After a moment he started searching around his seat for his packet of cigarettes.

"'ere," I said. "'ave one of mine," and I offered him my packet of Woodbines. He had a job to see where they were over the bandages and I placed them into his outstretched hand. Then he searched around for a box of matches.

"'ang on, I'll give you a light," I said, fumbling in my pocket for my matches.

"That's all right," he snapped back. "I'm not an invalid, you know. I can still light my own cigarettes."

But obviously he couldn't. He could strike the match but he misjudged the distance to the end of the cigarette and set fire to his dressing instead. Sally's mother let out a terrifying scream when she saw her husband's head being consumed by fire and did the only thing she could think of in the circumstances, and threw a jug of water over him.

So, now, to add to his misery, he not only had to change his shirt and trousers, he also had to remove and wring out the sopping wet dressing from his shattered nose, and replace it with a new makeshift dressing which turned out to be twice the size of the original. All this added disruption to a man already under stress didn't help the situation and when not long afterwards there was a knock on the front door announcing a visitor, Fred Evans, who was a driver on the railway, Sally's Dad wasn't in a particularly good frame of mind. Nevertheless we all shuffled round the small room to make a space for Fred to sit down.

"Someone's bin in the wars from the look of it," said Fred, which seemed a gross understatement. For a minute Sally's Dad didn't say anything. I suspected he didn't trust himself.

"I 'eard all about it. 'ow's it goin' then?" Fred persisted. He was a serious, quietly spoken man in his late fifties, and was obviously concerned with the sight which confronted him.

"Oh — not too bad," Dad said at last, after weighing up his words.

Even the large basket of elderberries which Fred had brought with him didn't seem to lift Dad's spirits. We all chatted for a while and then Sally's father asked, "Would yer like a drop of potato wine, Fred?"

"Why not?" his friend replied, smiling at the honour, and Dad eased himself out of his chair and went to the cupboard. After fossicking about for a couple of minutes, he eventually pulled out a couple of glasses with a bottle of wine.

"Not too much, Tom," said Sally's mother with a warning look as he poured a good measure into a glass.

Fred sipped the wine and commented how good it tasted as he emptied the glass.

"Ah — it's not a bad drop," agreed Sally's Dad, as he refilled Fred's glass.

I carefully lit another cigarette for Sally's Dad and he puffed away for a while, watching his visitor. Fred had started to relax now and was laughing affably, very different to when he first arrived.

"'ow about another drop?" he was asked.

"I don't think 'e should," said Sally's mother, looking concerned.

"Oh, 'e'll be all right — you feel all right, don't you, Fred?" asked Sally's Dad, obviously amused by Fred's transformation from a damp squid to the life and soul of the party — and seemingly forgetting about his broken nose and frizzy hair.

"Never felt better. That's pretty good stuff, your wine!" came his friend's cheerful reply.

"I know," said Dad, and he poured him another good measure.

Fred took his third glass and drank it down whilst Sally's mother looked more anxious by the minute. Then Fred suddenly turned to Sally and asked, "Can you sing?"

With that Sally's Mam stood up, grabbed the bottle and took it out of the room, saying to her husband:

"That's it, Tom — I told you 'e'd 'ad enough after the first glass!"

"Oh, 'e's all right — you're all right, aren't you, Fred?" asked Sally's Dad, and I caught a glimpse of a smile behind the bandage.

"Nothing wrong with me," answered Fred, suddenly letting out such a loud laugh that we all jumped.

"Per'aps it's time you were on your way," said Sally's mother, in a persuasive voice. "You've got a long ride 'ome to Sandhurst."

"That's true," said Fred, putting one hand on my shoulder to help himself stand up, and the other on the wall to keep him steady.

"Take care 'ow you go," said Sally's mother.

"I will, don't you worry about that," Fred responded, bumping into the door frame as he aimed for the passage, then getting lost in the coats hanging at the bottom of the stairs before finally locating the front door. "I'll be on my way then — see you all again soon!" were the last words we heard, before he closed the door behind him. We all sat quietly for a moment.

"I knew you shouldn't 'ave given 'im that second glass!" said Sally's mother, unable to contain herself anymore.

"Oh, 'e'll be all right — it was only a drop." The whole thing wickedly amused Sally's Dad. Then he had second thoughts and said to me, "Go and 'ave a look which way 'e went — and see if 'e's all right, Bill — just to be on the safe side."

I raced to the front gate. His bicycle was gone and when I looked towards Horton Road he was nowhere in sight. I hoped he was going to be all right. Near the top of Horton Road was a meeting of five roads and a person needed their wits about them when passing through that area.

"There you are," said Dad, afterwards. "If 'e could disappear up the road that fast, 'e couldn't 'ave been as drunk as you thought 'e was. You know, this lot of wine must be really good — my nose 'ardly 'urts at all now."

It didn't do Fred any good, though. The next day we heard that he had been arrested at the top of Horton Road for directing the traffic. Luckily his name was not printed in the newspaper otherwise he would have lost his job as a driver on the railways.

Fred never visited 130 Millbrook Street again.

CHAPTER
SEVEN

Lady

When spring came we bought Jill a new blue bicycle and she was keen to try it out. It wasn't her first two-wheeler. She'd had one before while I was still overseas, and apparently had tried to improve her riding skills by going "no-handed" round a corner, near Widden Street School, where the road had just been freshly sealed and there was plenty of loose stone about. Jill's bicycle skidded and she fell to the ground and ended up hobbling home with a lump of stone still embedded in her knee. Sally had already warned her to ride properly and to "act more ladylike", as she put it, but to no avail, and when this happened she took the bicycle off Jill and told her she was giving it away. In fact Mrs. Campbell hid it in the pub next door for about a week. By that time the bicycle's absence caused Jill such misery that Sally relented, only after Jill promised she would never try that stunt again.

Sally suggested we all take a ride to Stonebench, just under four miles away, to see the Severn Bore and christen the bike at the same time. The Severn Bore is a natural phenomenon where a large wave of water travels up the river from its estuary. The necessities for a good bore are high Spring tides — the biggest being near an equinox, when the day and night are of equal length — and a river estuary with the right shape to funnel the water into a slowly decreasing channel as it moves upstream.

We had spoken of the Bore at home, but Jill had never seen it, so it seemed a good opportunity for a family outing since we all enjoyed cycling and getting out into the countryside together.

I checked in the local newspaper for the estimated arrival time of the Bore at Stonebench and we all set off. We decided to go early and Sally made a flask of hot tea and some sandwiches to take with us. There were a couple of reasons for going earlier; first it was going to be a long way for Jill to ride so we wouldn't be able to ride as fast as Sally and I normally did, and secondly it was only an *estimated* time given that the Bore would pass through. A lot of things could either deter or hasten it on its journey, such as the way the wind was blowing, how much fresh water there was and the barometer reading.

I remember when I was a teenager and had ridden out to Stonebench with some mates. We judged that we would have about ten minutes to wait when we got there, but when we were only a short distance from the river we were met by hoards of people leaving the place.

They told us the good news: "You've just missed it".

It was a popular outing for Gloucester people every year. Stories abounded over the years about the individuals who had nearly drowned while trying to sail over it, swim through it, or escape from it — like the unsuspecting fisherman from another part of the country who I heard about. He was completely unaware of any such thing as a bore and had been peacefully sitting on the lower part of the river bank close to the water somewhere upstream, no doubt minding his own business and enjoying his peaceful surroundings, when suddenly he heard a roar and found this huge wall of water bearing down on him. He had only seconds to throw himself over the top of the riverbank before the water roared past, taking all his belongings with it.

These stories were retold each year as people set off to see the event. And in the telling, excitement grew. Would the Bore be a good one this year or would it be nothing more than a big swell, when we would all come away disappointed and say what a wasted journey it had been? Or would it be a "big un"? Or would we witness somebody trying to swim through it and we could all stand on the river bank, shaking our heads and call out "silly bugger" — secretly wishing we had half the nerve to try it ourselves? For all the times I saw it I never, ever, saw anybody in the water, so I have to admit that that side of it was a bit disappointing for me.

The weather that day was what you might expect for spring. We woke to the sound of rain on the bedroom window panes, but by the time we finished breakfast it had stopped and the clouds had started to clear. As we rode along Barton Street the sun broke through although the air was still chilly. There wasn't much traffic along the Bristol Road and in a short time we had turned off into one of the country lanes, which eventually led to Stonebench. When we arrived at our destination there were already a few people waiting and we found a good viewpoint high up on the grassy riverbank. The wind seemed much colder now we were near the water and we huddled round as Sally poured us all a cup of hot tea.

Below us the river glided past and we watched it disappear round a bend a little further downstream. Submerged objects caused small swirls here and there on the surface of the brown-coloured water. Soon more people arrived and within an hour a big crowd had gathered, with bicycles everywhere. People began looking earnestly downstream as the arrival time drew near. Fathers put their small children on their shoulders for a better view and suddenly we heard the roar of the water in the distance, getting louder and louder, sending a charge through everybody:

"I can 'ear it comin'."

"Look - yer 'tis."

" 'ennit big!"

"Blimey! — *Stand back — stand back!*"

"Look at the size of it!"

" 'ang on ter yer bikes!"

"I'm all wet!"

"WE KNOW THAT ALREADY!"

— then it was gone . . .

The Bore was extra high that day, spraying up above the banks in several places, adding to the overall effect. Nobody was disappointed, except for the few who stood too close and got drenched, and Jill, who thought it didn't last long enough. After such a long ride she hadn't expected the whole thing to be over in less than a minute, but that's the way Bores are. You see it coming - it roars past - then it's gone.

The general opinion, however, was that the journey had been worth it.

As we were riding along on our way home, we saw that one of the hedgerows on the side of the lane was covered in blackberries, so we stopped to pick some. After a couple of minutes I heard a man's voice calling out from the other side of the hedge.

"There's a lot more berries over this side," he said. "Why don't you send your little maid over here to get them?"

I thanked him and told Jill to go through the five-bar gate close by and pick them on the other side of the hedge, opposite to me, so that I could still see her. A few minutes later I saw her bending down, talking and laughing and then she was walking back through the gate. In her arms was a beautiful little black and white puppy.

"They seem to like each other," laughed the farmer, as the puppy tried to lick Jill all over her face. "I'll give her the little puppy, if yer like — it's the last of a litter."

Jill looked pleadingly at me, but I hesitated. There was going to be a bit of a problem. I wanted to take it, my family had always had a dog and I loved them, but Sally's family had never had a dog and they weren't particularly keen on them. Perhaps I could persuade Sally, I thought, and looked to see where she was, but she was too far away along the lane.

"Is it a male or female?" I asked the farmer, thinking that would help me make a final decision.

"It's a female," he answered.

We'd always had males. My grandfather reckoned that females were a nuisance because of their unwanted litters. Just then Sally returned and asked what was happening and when she heard about the puppy she was adamant that we should not take it.

"Put it down, love," she said to Jill. "We haven't got room for a dog in our house. Besides, Gong Gong wouldn't like one for a start."

Jill reluctantly put the puppy on the ground by her feet.

"I'm sorry," I said to the farmer, "we won't be able to take it."

"That's a shame, but never mind, sooner or later I'll find a home for her," he said.

With that Sally rode off ahead believing that was the end of the matter — and it would have been if the farmer hadn't given his best parting shot.

"I'll tell you somethin'," he said. "Whoever gets that dog'll 'ave a good 'un. My neighbour's dog was the father and mine was the mother, and they're the best farm dogs in the area."

Those few words sealed the matter. A good farm dog would be good at catching rats, I thought, and if I was going to get some pigs — like I planned in the near future — there was sure to be rats around and I would need a good dog. That was as good a reason as any, I thought. It could validate her place in the family. I quickly turned round and scooped up the puppy, and placed it inside my shirt.

"Not a word," I said to Jill who willingly entered into the conspiracy. We thanked the farmer, and he smiled warmly and wished us luck as we rode off to catch up with Sally.

Miraculously the puppy stayed hidden inside my shirt and jacket and hardly moved. My clothes weren't tight so there was plenty of room, and formed a kind of hammock for her to lie in. Perhaps the dog knew its future depended upon being quiet — and I hoped that she was house-trained. It wasn't until we were on the outskirts of Gloucester that the puppy decided to pop her fluffy head out through the neck of my shirt to see what was going on, just at the same time that Sally was talking to me. She was struck dumb for a couple of seconds — but soon recovered. Luckily the traffic was pretty busy at that spot on the road and certainly not the place to stop and have a row about the fate of a poor defenceless little animal, so we cycled on until we got into a side street, nearer home, before she spoke about it.

"Where are we going to keep a dog? There won't be enough room!" she said, with a hopeless look on her face.

"Don't worry about that. I'll build a kennel. Besides," I said, hoping to ease the situation, "it's going to be a good rat-catcher."

"RATS? WHAT RATS? WE HAVEN'T GOT RATS!"

"I know — I know," I said quickly trying to calm her down, half expecting people to start opening their front doors along the street to see what all the fuss was about. "But when I get some pigs . . ." I said.

Sally sighed and rolled her eyes. "I don't know what Dad's going to make of it all."

It wasn't long before we found out. When we arrived home Jill was already in the house with the puppy before Sally and I had time to put the bicycles away and we heard her grandfather's response while we were still outside.

"We don't want that thing in 'ere!" he said.

"It's mine, Gong Gong. We got it from a farmer — he gave it to me," said Jill, full of excitement.

"Well — you can take it back, then!" he said. "You must all want yer 'eads looked at, bringing that thing in 'ere!"

We told him how we came to have it, how Jill wanted it, what the farmer had said and my plans for it — but it was no use. He was adamant.

"Never 'ad one — never wanted one — dirty things!"

Then, whether the puppy got over-excited with all the raised voices, or felt it should do what was expected, it squatted down and left a neat little puddle on the carpet right in front of him!

After such a disgraceful beginning, the puppy and Dad eyed each other with caution over the next few days. Slowly the ball of fur charmed its way into his life and within a couple of weeks it was walking by Dad's side up to the allotments — the best of mates. We called her "Lady".

CHAPTER
EIGHT

Ratting

A friend of mine named Frank Simpson had a ferret and was keen to put its skills to the test. He asked me if I was interested in going along with him to catch rats, and since it was at the time when I was in need of a live rat to familiarise Lady with at close quarters, I agreed. I had already been keeping pigs for a while by now, buying weaners about six weeks old from the market and selling them five months later as fat stock. This had been made possible when a piece of land big enough for a smallholding and conveniently adjacent to the pathway to the Tea Bridge had become available — and I had grabbed it with both hands. The field next to it belonged to Mr. Ravenhill from Windmill Parade, the man who kindly gave Jill eggs during the war.

There wasn't a shortage of rats around the pigsties, either. The problem was that Lady would chase them a lot, but never caught one and treated the whole episode as a bit of fun. She was well past the puppy stage and approaching the age when her hereditary instincts should have started emerging. With the right encouragement, I thought, she might get serious on helping to keep the rodent population down. It was clear that she was an intelligent dog and keen to learn. She was already good friends with all the other gardeners since she quickly learned not to walk on their gardens but only on the paths around them. She would stand up on her back legs to look around and get her bearings if she could hear one of us whistle but couldn't see where we were. Providing she could hear the whistle she would find you. It didn't matter how far away she was, once she had the correct direction she would race, zigzag, along the paths in between the allotments to her destination, stopping a couple of times to pop up again on her hind legs to check her progress and direction.

Sometimes Jill would whistle to her when she was on the top of the Tea Bridge and she would watch Lady stand up and look around. Jill would wave her hands and whistle again and off the dog would go weaving her way through the gardens until she reached the gate and then tear up the path towards the bridge where she would be warmly praised for being so clever.

Frank and I met late one afternoon and set off for a place not far away, where there was a small brook. Both of us wore the obligatory overalls and big wellington boots. I also took along a box to carry home a couple of live rats, if we were lucky, so that Lady could have a closer introduction, and Frank carried his ferret and the nets. Less than twenty minutes later we were standing on the bank of the stream viewing the territory. On the farther side of it we could see lots of rat holes. It promised to be a fruitful exercise.

"Should get a good catch 'ere," said Frank with relish, as he placed his ferret's cage on the ground and unpacked his nets. It was the first time I had gone ratting with a ferret and he quickly explained to me how the nets were placed over all the rat holes except one. Then the ferret was placed down the last hole, which was then filled in behind it so that it couldn't get back out. As the animal went down through the tunnels the rats would try to escape through the various exits — straight into the nets. He didn't say what we were expected to do with all the rats if there were a lot of them. Carefully we laid the nets over all the holes along the bank except for one on the top of it, and then Frank stood at the clear entrance with the ferret in his hand.

"Are they all covered now, Bill?"

I did a last minute scan from where I was standing in the middle of the brook. It was barely three foot wide at this point and the water was only up to my ankles. "Looks all right to me," I said.

"'ere goes, then," Frank said, released the ferret down the hole and closed the hole behind it. We both eagerly watched the nets, waiting for something to happen. Suddenly, like ping pong balls shooting out of a ball dispenser, a rat shot out of a hole right in front of me — a hole we had missed with the net. Followed by another, and another, and another. Plopping out into the water, one after the other they skimmed across the brook on either side of my feet. Nearly falling back into the water myself, I flayed about with the shock of it! Then they were all gone. We only captured one rat in a net that day so at least the ferret was happy.

70

The following week I managed to catch a live one in a cage trap at the pigsties and followed the five steps my grandfather had told me about years earlier.

1. Find a large tub and put the rat in it.
2. Place the dog in the tub as well.
3. Dog plays with rat.
4. Rat doesn't want to play — and bites dog on nose.
5. Dog despatches unfriendly playmate.

It happened exactly as predicted and certainly unlocked Lady's instinctive capabilities. After that she killed all the rats that crossed her path — skilfully too.

I remember once when I discovered that half the food in the pigs' troughs was being eaten by the rodents instead of the pigs and realised that something had to be done about it, quickly. So after feeding the pigs one afternoon and watching them retire afterwards for a slumber on their clean straw bed, I sat in the sty with Lady by my side, and waited. She never moved and I never spoke, we just sat there dead still, my hand gently resting on her neck. We both had our eyes on the holes where we knew the rats were coming from.

After what seemed an eternity but in all probability was only a couple of minutes, I saw a rat pop its head out to check if it was clear then disappear again. It was a usual cautionary manoeuvre. The pigs were snoring happily by now. I never moved, but I felt a faint quiver of excitement beneath my hand and knew Lady was waiting for my signal to give chase. Still we waited, and still she remained focused. Again a rat popped its head out and looked around. This time it made a run for the trough, followed by a few more. Lady was almost bursting with tension now and when I lifted my hand she attacked, killing about three of them — and I got one with a spade — the rest got away.

It wasn't long afterwards that my rabbit gave birth to the most beautiful litter. I had several rabbit hutches set apart from the pigsties and Jill was completely enchanted by the new arrivals, visiting them every day, feeding them and watching the tiny things grow into balls of white and brown fluff, the same colouring as their mother.

Then one morning I went to feed them and found all the babies dead — mutilated and partly eaten. The poor mother lay exhausted at one end of her hutch with pieces of fur missing from all over her. She must have put up a gallant fight for her babies, but without success. On inspection I could see that the rats had gnawed away at the edge of the wooden hutch where the wire mesh was attached, and had squeezed in underneath it. Then I remembered - it was spring and the rats needed food for their young. How cruel nature could be in its fight for survival, I thought.

That morning I was so angry that I went round the ground filling up any holes I could find and stamping on them. Lady became all excited as she sensed that "battle was about to commence" and sure enough, as I filled up more and more holes, a rat here and there would take flight and she would have it. We worked well that day, Lady and I, and at least it made me feel better by the end of it. The doe recovered, but afterwards breeding rabbits didn't have the same appeal.

Another of Lady's innate farm skills came to light some time later. I had built some chicken pens in the back of 130 Millbrook Street and soon we were having fresh-laid eggs every day. Then after a while they stopped laying, like birds do from time to time. I remember thinking it a bit strange at the time, because we had heard the hens clucking like they do when they have laid an egg, but when we checked later there was usually nothing there. Not long afterwards Sally remarked how well Lady was looking.

"You know that dog's got a beautiful shiny coat," she said. "Look how thick and shiny it is."

We all agreed. I hadn't seen a better looking coat on any other dog and she was bursting with so much energy that we congratulated ourselves on obviously feeding her a good diet. Then a suspicion suddenly dawned on me and I went to her kennel and tipped it out. Sure enough, dozens of empty egg shells fell out on to the ground.

I knew I had to catch her in the act if I wanted to stop her doing it, so I patiently waited by the window inside the house and watched her kennel. After a while there was the sound of a chicken clucking, letting everybody know that she had laid an egg. The next thing Lady was out of her kennel and running up to the nesting boxes. I quickly slipped out of the scullery door into the yard, quick enough to see her lift the lid with her nose and put her head inside. When she pulled her head out she was holding an egg in her mouth. She let the lid fall back down and was sneakily running back to her kennel when she spotted me standing in the back yard. She put the egg on the ground and raced to her kennel, but I got there first and grabbed her by the scruff of the neck and shook her vigorously and scolded her. After that I put a latch on the nesting boxes — and her fur never looked quite as good ever again.

Many years later when I would talk about Lady and how clever she was, my grandson would say jokingly, "Oh, you mean 'Lady the Wonder Dog'."

I couldn't have put it better myself.

CHAPTER NINE

Sollars's Field

After I fed the pigs and other animals one Saturday afternoon, I decided to walk over to our allotment to pick some peas and dig up a few potatoes for our Sunday dinner. Our vegetable patch, which was one of about forty, was on the far edge of all the plots and next to a large field of about six acres belonging to Mr. Sollars.

The thing that made Mr. Sollars's field different from Mr. Ravenhill's land and my smallholding was that it had its own access through a tunnel on the far side, which ran beneath the railway lines, allowing Mr. Sollars to move his cattle in and out of his field whenever he liked, without any difficulty. It was different for Mr. Ravenhill and myself. When he wanted to bring his horse to his field or I needed to bring my pigs to their sties, we had to walk them past the Foundry, down through the tunnel, and then, if none of them had escaped by then, through one of the side gates onto a railway line and along the path to their destination. Other problems arose if you were suddenly confronted by a pedestrian or cyclist coming the other way. Besides all that, it was a feat that normally required more than one person to accomplish. So, in many ways I envied Mr. Sollars. How easy it must be, I thought, to look after your animals with that kind of set up. I soon learned, however, that some people don't know when they are well off.

On reaching the pigsties that afternoon I quickly made their feed up. The pigs always knew when it was feed time and let everybody in the area know it as well. From the moment they heard the sound of the buckets of food being prepared their snuffled grunts would turn to loud squeals as expectations grew. I had built a shed next to the sties where I boiled up the vegetable scraps from home and generous neighbours in a large boiler. In return I would repay with an egg here and there, just as Mr. Ravenhill had done with Jill during the war.

Meal and cod liver oil were added to the warm cooked vegetables and in the winter an extra couple of spoonfuls of oil "to keep the cold out". The animals loved it and some of them proved to be cleverer than the rest once they got a taste for it. Whilst most would squeal hysterically and carry on as if they hadn't been fed for a week, with lots of pushing and shoving to get to the trough, even though there was always room for them to feed side by side if they so chose, there was always one who avoided the squabbles. That one would quietly walk to the trough and wait until the oil came to the surface of the swill and suck it all off the top, more or less before the rest had sorted themselves out. When that happened I'd have to drizzle some more directly over the trough and hope they all got some. No wonder

Sally joked to people: "'e looks after 'is pigs better than us sometimes!"

After feeding all the animals I walked further on to our allotment, where I was amazed to see six half-grown calves being chased over all the other allotments by Harry Massey, who grew vegetables next to us. He was an old man in his late seventies who lived with his wife in Alfred Street, and was certainly not in any condition for such exertion.

He was a great mate of Sally's father and normally a cheerful bloke with a ready smile, but today, as he continued waving his cloth cap in the air, I could see he was having difficulties. Harry stopped to get his breath back, his normal florid complexion much redder now — verging on purple. He wiped his eyes with his handkerchief, and then he lifted his cap and wiped his brow.

"'ang on, 'arry," I called out. "Take your time — I'll give yer a 'and."

I managed to shoo a couple of the calves back towards the other four who had taken a liking to somebody's cabbage patch.

"Where the 'ell did this lot come from?" I asked, wondering if they'd somehow escaped from a railway wagon, and if so, what we were going to do with them.

"From Sollars's field," Harry gasped.

"No wonder they look fit and 'ealthy," I said.

"The bloody things are always getting out. They eat all the stuff off our gardens."

Harry pointed out the broken fence a short distance away. The whole fence looked a bit makeshift now that I had a good look.

"'ave yer told Mr. Sollars about it?" I asked.

"Many times — but it's no good telling that bloke. All yer ever get is — 'e's sorry!"

Once Harry had recovered, we slowly drove the calves back into the field and I made a quick repair to the fence before leaving. When I returned home I mentioned the episode to Dad and he confirmed Harry's story.

"I must 'ave lost 'alf of my stuff over the past six months to 'is animals," he said

"You've never said anything," I said, wishing I had known something about it before. The pigs had kept me busy and Dad more or less handled the allotment, except for the heavy digging which I always did. I hadn't worried about it because he loved being up his allotment where he could do a bit of gardening if he felt like it or chat with his mates.

"Not much point in saying anything," he said. "What can we do about it?"

"Somebody should 'ave a serious word with this Mr. Sollars," I said, feeling nettled by the whole affair. The people who worked on those allotments included a lot of elderly people, who relied on the vegetables they grew there. This man was treating the gardeners with contempt. He already annoyed me and I hadn't even met the man.

"You're wasting yer time, Bill," said Dad.

"But it's Sollars's duty to fence his animals in — it's his fault," I persisted.

"You try telling 'im that," said Dad.

"Don't worry, I'm going to," I said, all fired up and ready to go. "Where does 'e live?"

"'e lives in the first 'ouse in Upton Lane," said Dad.

"Right, I'm off to see 'im," I said, grabbing my coat out of the hallway.

"I'm telling yer it's a waste of time," Dad called out to me. "Yer won't get any change out of 'im!"

"If I don't try, I won't know," I yelled back before closing the front door.

It was about half an hour's bicycle ride to Upton Lane and I quickly located the house, a large detached place standing in about a quarter of an acre of well-kept lawns and rose gardens. I put my bicycle against the wall outside and walked up the driveway. Near the house was a fellow bending over some rose trees. He had his back to me.

"Excuse me," I called out, "does Mr. Sollars live here?"

The man turned round and we both stared at each other for a second.

"Bloody hell, haven't seen you for years — Bill Lawrence, isn't it?"

"That's right," I recognized him now, "and you're George Sollars, right?"

He nodded his head. I knew him from before the war, when we had worked together, and also remembered that he had a reputation for being a "boss's man", a sort of yes-sir-no-sir kind of chap, which had not gone down well with his work mates.

"What brings you here, Bill?" he asked.

"I was under the impression that the man I am looking for is a lot older than you, George," I said. "I'm 'ere about some calves that keep getting out of a field, next to some railway allotments and eating off the gardens."

"Oh, that's the old man you want to see. I'll call him," he said and disappeared into the house. I waited and waited, wondering how long it could possibly take to tell a person that there was someone to see them, and long enough for me to think about knocking on the front door to see what was going on. If he thought I might just give up and leave, he would have to think again.

Then an older man came out of the house. He was a heavily built man with a brusque manner and a handlebar moustache, which had been carefully waxed. Dad's words: "you won't get any change out of him" echoed through my mind. Looking at him I believed it, and from his manner it was obvious I was an unwelcome visitor. So, "taking the bull by the horns", although I would rather have "taken the man by his moustache", I introduced myself.

"Mr. Sollars," I said, holding out my hand, "I 'aven't 'ad the pleasure of meeting you before. My name is Bill Lawrence." He reluctantly shook it and mumbled a curt reply, his hand feeling like a limp piece of meat. Then I told him the purpose of my visit.

"Yes," he said. "My son has told me about it. I am very sorry about this, but you can rest assured that the fence will be repaired tomorrow. My sons are not working on Sundays so they will attend to it." He sounded convincing and with that promise I thanked him and headed home.

When I arrived home Dad asked: "What did 'e say then?"

I opened my mouth to reply, but before I could say a word he continued. "No, let me tell you. He said 'Sorry about that, but my sons will repair the fence tomorrow', right?"

"That's right, that's what 'e said, almost word for word," I said, suddenly feeling riled. If Mr. Sollars thought he could give me the "run-around" and get away with it, he had better think again. I would not let the problem drop now — it needed sorting out once and for all.

"You've wasted yer time, Bill," said Dad.

"Well, 'e'd better repair that fence or there'll be trouble."

I heard no more about invading cattle over the next couple of weeks, and since Dad was up the allotments nearly every day I presumed that Mr. Sollars had done the right thing and everything was sorted out. So when I visited the garden on a Saturday afternoon about a fortnight later to dig up some more potatoes, I was surprised to see a commotion taking place on another garden next to ours.

"Bill, those bloody animals are over 'ere, again," shouted Fred Lane. He was about the same age as me and grew a good variety of vegetables for his family of four. Sure enough there were the same six calves, slightly bigger now, strolling across the garden plots, nibbling as they went. It infuriated me that Mr. Sollars thought he could get away with it. I decided it was about time he was taught a lesson he wouldn't forget!

"Help me drive the animals down past my pigs, towards the gate," I called out to Fred.

"What? You mean the one through into the footpath?" asked Fred, suddenly looking worried.

"That's right. After that you can leave them to me."

"What you going to do?" Fred asked and for a moment I thought he was going to baulk at the idea. He looked around to see if there would be any witnesses, but there were none.

"Don't worry — you'll find out later," I said.

It didn't take long, five minutes at the most, and once I had the calves through the gate into the alley I steadily drove them along it and into the subway under the railway lines at the end of it, then past the foundry on the other side. After that I drove them down Windmill Parade to the Horton Road crossing. The fellow in the signal box, unaware that he was aiding a misdemeanour, lifted the gates and I shooed the cattle across on to the Horton Road.

Then I went home.

I knew the cattle would be quickly impounded because the cattle yards were only a short distance away, and sat back and waited for the repercussions. The following Wednesday a notice appeared in the local paper:

STRAYING CATTLE IMPOUNDED.
OWNER MAY CLAIM AFTER PAYING KEEP
EXPENSES.

About a week later I was having a drink in my local when George Sollars came in.

"That wasn't very clever, Bill, what you did last week," he said.

"What was that, then?" I asked innocently.

"Letting those calves out on to the main road. They were impounded and it cost the old man fifteen quid to get them out."

"I don't know what you're on about," I said. "Anyway, your old man promised that the fence would be repaired, and if your Dad's calves got out again and wandered down the alley and eventually out on to the main road . . . well . . . Oh George, I do hope your Dad is repairing the fence now." I couldn't help the sarcasm creeping into my voice.

"There won't be any more livestock out there again until that fence is solid and secure, I can assure you of that," replied George, and then he burst out laughing. "You should have seen the old man's face when he read the paper and realised it was his calves. I thought he was going to explode. Go on, drink up — have the next one on me. You saved our kid and me a job with that fence. The old man's coughing up and having a real job done by a contractor."

After that the gardens were safe from the cattle but not from the rabbits.

CHAPTER TEN

Mr Gaze

Jill had moved into Mr. Gaze's class at Widden Street School in preparation for sitting the 11-plus examination and the possibility of obtaining a place at one of the two local High Schools if she did well enough. Consequently, there was much talk and encouragement at home about her working hard over the next twelve months and achieving this goal.

"Just imagine," Sally would say, brimming with pride at the thought of it, "if you pass you could go to Denmark Road High School for Girls and wear their lovely uniform. It's a navy blue gymslip with a cross over top, a blue and white striped shirt with a navy, red and green striped tie. It looks really smart."

"But I like the colours of Ribston Hall better — green and yellow," Jill said.

"Forget the colours," I said, seeing the discussion getting away from the main objective. "The first thing is to pass the exam, then we'll see which one you go to afterwards." Even if we were asked for our school preferences, I wasn't sure if we had much of a choice. In the end a child would be sent to a school the Government deemed suitable.

Widden Street Junior School was a two-storey red brick building situated in Sinope Street, about a five minutes walk from home. On the other side, across the playground, was a primary school.

At first sight Mr. Gaze was rather a formidable looking man and I could understand how half the children were scared of him, Jill included, from what she told me. He was a tall, gaunt man somewhere in his late forties, with sharp features and brown bead-like eyes. His black hair looked suspiciously dark for his age, especially around his temples where a few grey hairs would have been expected, but were absent. And gauging from the strong nicotine stains on his fingers he smoked a lot outside of school.

Hardly any of the children played up in his class, and those who did were quickly dealt a few whacks of his cane. As I soon found out, girls who misbehaved, such as Jill, were sent to Mrs. Jennings who carried out the punishment with a ruler. Perhaps he worked at keeping his stern appearance, because it certainly worked. Surprisingly though, I found him to be a very agreeable man when we spoke, someone who genuinely loved his work and was good at it if the results from the previous years were to be believed. Nearly all his students would pass every year, giving Widden Street School a good reputation. I hoped Jill was going to be one of the lucky ones now she was in his class.

When I approached him and said I was Jill's father and asked how Sally and I could help, he said how pleased he was to see me and wished that other parents would do the same.

"I'm sure Jill can do it," he said. "The trouble is she gets her head filled up with comics and all that sort of rubbish. If you cut out all that stuff at home, I'll do my best here and with any luck she'll get through." He went on to tell me why she had received the cane. It was for passing notes in class, when she had already been warned not to.

That night we had a good throw out of comics and any other items deemed to be distracting. Naturally there were lots of tears — but we had a good talk about whether she wanted to go to a high school or not. She said she did and it was eventually agreed that she wasn't going to get there if she didn't try, so we ended up with new resolutions being made.

As the months passed I checked back with Mr. Gaze and he said things were progressing nicely, that Jill was definitely improving and to keep up the good work. Although she was scared of him Jill also liked him because he always had a session for drawing once a week and she had always liked drawing. One day she brought home her artwork to show us. Sally was quite taken aback by the subject chosen, because he had asked the class to make up a name for a pub and design its sign. She thought children should be pointed in another direction. But from what Jill told us all the children in his class enthusiastically entered the challenge, resulting in astonishing names for their signs. Even the most inapt artists in the class were keen to put their ideas on paper. He certainly knew how to connect — in more ways than one — with his students, and that was probably the secret of his success.

Then one Saturday morning, as summer approached, Jill asked me if I had a spare sack anywhere. I asked her what it was for.

" 'Old Gazer' showed us a plant at school," she said.

"I hope you don't call him that!" I said, secretly thinking of the names I had called my teachers in the past.

" 'Course not!" she said with a shocked look, fearing I might think she was so stupid.

"What do you want the sack for, then?"

"Well," Jill said, enthusiastically, "he asked us if we knew where the plant was growing wild. I told him there was lots of it up by the allotments, and he asked if I could take him some."

"But you don't need a sack — just take him a bit in a paper bag," I said.

"No," she said. "He said a bunch of it would be nice. So I want to take him a big bunch — there's stacks of it up there."

She was obviously getting along well with Mr. Gaze, so I handed over the sack to her. I didn't want to break up a good teacher-pupil relationship.

Over the weekend she scrounged another sack off her grandfather and when she set off for school on Monday she was carrying two huge sackfuls of the stuff. Luckily they weren't heavy, just bulky. That night when we sat around having tea I asked her what Mr. Gaze thought of the sacks.

"He was surprised!" she said smiling proudly.

I bet he was, I thought.

"I took the most."

"I thought you might 'ave," said Dad, completely bewildered by anyone wanting a bag of weeds, especially a schoolteacher.

"Did he say what he wanted it for?" I asked.

"No," said Jill. "But somebody said at playtime that they thought he dried it and smoked it."

Sally, her father, and I looked at each other across the table — but said nothing.

As the 11-plus exam loomed closer I asked my brother Wally to come and give Jill any last minute tips he could think of to help. We had already bought some mock examination sheets from a place in Birmingham, and they had been quite useful. Wally was the brainy one in the family and had won a scholarship to a boys' High School in Gloucester when he was about Jill's age. All of us were really proud of him; he was the first member of the family to have achieved such a thing. But Dad had said he couldn't afford to send him there, so he didn't go.

Wally went over several things with Jill, general things on how to approach the questions, how to keep calm and how to be methodical about it. We all believed his final touch helped Jill achieve her goal. And much to the family's delight, she was given a place at Denmark Road High School for Girls.

CHAPTER
ELEVEN

The Missing Beans

After the retired railwaymen had finished gardening for the day, you would always find them sunning themselves on benches outside their allotment sheds. Such was the day I found Dad sitting and enjoying his Woodbine. By his side was his mate, Fred Ridge, a retired railway driver, puffing away at his pipe, both of them enjoying the last burst of an Indian summer. The clear blue sky above was marred only by a few wisps of cloud in the distance. Dad, Fred and their mutual friend, Harry Massey, spent most of their time gardening and sitting in the sunshine, if there was any about.

"I thought I'd better pick those beans before the frost gets 'em," I said, indicating a patch further along our allotment.

"Good idea," said Dad. "This weather can't last much longer."

"I 'eard 'arry Massey 'ad a few onions taken off 'is patch," said Fred. "'ave yer seen anybody 'anging about?"

"No," I said. "But that's one of the risks we take with these allotments, isn't it? There's always somebody ready to help themselves."

"I wish I could get my 'ands on 'em," said Dad.

"Same 'ere," agreed Fred, puffing on his pipe vigorously for a few seconds as his mind worked overtime. "I was in the Plough last night, 'aving a pint with 'arry, and 'e reckons them foundry blokes are the culprits. They're on shift work and are going through the footpath all 'ours of the day and night."

"Could be," said Dad. "Or it could be railway blokes — remember, they're on shift work as well."

"Ah ..." said Fred, thoughtfully, and again big puffs of smoke escaped from the corner of his mouth. They fell silent for a while and I wandered along to the bean patch, leaving them to the thoughts of old men. As I neared the bean sticks it struck me that the foliage on them looked a bit thin and on further investigation I found out why. There wasn't one bean in sight — it had been stripped bare.

"Someone's had the lot!" I yelled back to them and the next thing they were both shuffling along the path towards me. Dad was soon checking along the rows, hardly believing that someone had been so thorough and getting angrier by the second as he realised what I had said was true.

"What a bloody nerve!" said Fred, looking with disbelief.

Meanwhile Dad was bending down and appeared to be searching for something between the plants.

"'ang on," he said, picking up something from the ground. "What 'ave we got 'ere?"

90

He held a large leather wallet in his hand, and Fred and I gathered round him as he opened it to see who it belonged to.

"Well, well, 'ow's that for a bit of luck?" said Dad, bursting with laughter. "Five quid, and the bloke's name to go with it — 'is name's Jack 'ammonds."

"Jack 'ammonds?" Fred repeated the name several times, running it through the memory files in his brain before it suddenly connected. "Blimey! I know 'im. 'e don't work at the Foundry, 'e's a Railway Inspector. And I know where we can find 'im. 'e uses the Red Lion every Sunday morning."

Dad was really enjoying himself now. "Five quid for a few beans — *and* we know who the thief is. 'ow about you and me go to the Red Lion for a pint on Sunday morning, Fred?"

"Wait a minute, Tom, what do you intend doing if 'e's there?" asked Fred with a look of apprehension on his face.

"Nothing for you to worry about," Dad said, smiling. "Oh, I'm really going to enjoy this. In the meantime, though, let's keep this to ourselves. I don't want anything to upset our Sunday drink."

Dad didn't have to worry though. From the look on Fred's face he would be too frightened to say anything to anybody anywhere.

"What about you, Bill? You going to come too?" Dad asked me. I occasionally went next door to the Windmill for a pint with him, otherwise we generally drank with our own mates. The way things were going

91

this time, however, I began to think it might be a good idea if I was around in case he got himself into trouble.

As arranged, we made our way to the Red Lion the following Sunday where the Public Bar already had most of its usual customers. We got our drinks and found a table with a good view of the bar and sat down.

"Don't recognise some of these blokes," said Tom in a low voice. "Is 'e 'ere yet?"

"No," said Fred, quickly sipping his beer. Then holding his glass in front of his mouth in case someone might lip-read him, he whispered: "Don't worry, I'll let you know when 'e's 'ere."

Several more customers dribbled into the place and each time we looked towards Fred for a sign, but he gave none. Then about ten minutes later a man came into the pub on his own. He was a smartly dressed man in a grey lounge suit who would have looked more at ease in the Lounge Bar of a hotel or club. Fred gave us a nudge and puffed a vigorous smokescreen from his pipe before saying from the corner of his mouth: "That's 'im standing at the bar now."

The man was not the sort you would expect to find in this type of pub in this part of town. Besides, what was an Inspector drinking in a place like this for? Was he trying to pick up some gossip from some of the railway workers who didn't know him? If he was he was doing a bad job of blending in.

"What're yer going to do?" asked Fred, nervously.

"Watch me," said Dad, with a twinkle in his eye. Fred did as he was told, his pipe no longer alight but clenched between his teeth as he sat in frozen terror. We watched Dad casually approach the bar and stand next to the Inspector. The man, sensing his presence, turned to him and they nodded agreeably to each other, the same as any drinkers may do when they go down to the local pub for a quiet Sunday drink. Fred and I waited. What did Dad have in mind, we wondered? He hadn't said anything to me about his plans. Then Dad took the wallet from his jacket pocket and flashed it around in the air, in full view of everyone, like a magician does at the start of a trick.

"What's up with Tom?" somebody asked us.

"We don't know," Fred and I chorused. It was the truth, we didn't.

Once he had everybody's attention, which didn't take long since anyone acting this strangely with their wallet in a public bar is immediately the focus of attention, he opened it and removed the five pound note and held it high in the air between his fingers.

"Landlord," Dad said loudly, "drinks all round, and the bloke who owns this wallet — if he would like to claim it . . ." Dad turned it around in the air so that everybody could see it. The Inspector standing next to him glanced up at the wallet and then looked again. We saw his face drain of colour and he turned back quickly to his drink. The room went quiet as everybody waited for the owner to come forward. Even a pin would have been heard — if it had been dropped. Dad turned to the Inspector. He didn't speak. The Inspector looked again at him and this time the thief knew he had been rumbled when he looked at Dad's face.

Someone called out: "Are you all right, Tom? Thought you'd won the Pools for a minute!" and everyone laughed. Then everybody quickly called out their orders to the barman in case Dad had second thoughts.

The Inspector took advantage of the diversion and swallowed his drink and left.

Later, as we left the pub, a more relaxed Fred chuckled over the morning's events.

"That was a clever move, Tom, what you did just now," he said, with obvious admiration for his old mate. "You knew 'e wouldn't claim the wallet, didn't you?"

"That's right," said Dad. "And I bet he won't go near our gardens again, either!"

CHAPTER
TWELVE

Holidays

The year following the war we decided to go for a holiday and after much discussion settled on Weymouth. We had never been there before but had heard good reports of the place and set about finding a hotel not far from the seafront. In the end our search was rewarded with a small hotel only two streets back from the promenade and still within our budget for bed, breakfast and evening meal. We considered ourselves lucky.

The Beamans lived four doors away from us, next to Barnes's shop and we had already asked Vi and Len Beaman if they would let their daughter, Joan, about the same age and a friend of Jill's, come with us and they agreed. Len was a slaughterman at the local abattoir and had a fine reputation of being very good at his job. He was also keen on a beer or two, to the extent that it was rumoured that his bicycle could find its own way home, like a horse returning to its stable, when he over-indulged. By nature he was a very happy, gentle person, with a cheerful word for everybody and I often wondered if having a beer was the way he coped with his job.

I can't remember exactly how many children they had — there were definitely three girls — and the youngest was a lovely little boy named John, who they had both longed for. He was good-looking with the same gentle nature as his father.

"Wouldn't say boo to a goose," Vi would say, looking at her youngest child lovingly.

Her comment was fully illustrated one day when Sally was visiting her. John must have been about five or six years old at the time. Vi was in the midst of telling Sally a story when John gently pulled on his mother's skirt, interrupting her.

"Mam," he said, looking up at her.

"Not now, John," Vi said, dismissing him and carrying on with her story.

"But, Mam," he said, his dear little face looking quite anxious.

"I said, not now, John," his mother said, trying to show patience while at the same time teaching her son good manners. She continued her conversation.

"Please, Mam," said John, now almost crying, his bottom lip quivering.

"WHAT IS IT?"

"You're standing on my foot," he whimpered.

"OH, MY POOR LITTLE LAMB!" Vi was so overcome with remorse that she picked him up and cradled him in her arms like a newborn baby, smothering him with kisses. "I WOULDN'T 'URT YOU FOR ALL THE TEA IN CHINA!" she said, nuzzling a kiss into his neck, making him break out in a fit of giggles. Suddenly he was smiling again.

★ ★ ★

Fortunately the weather was very good at Weymouth for the whole week. If it had rained during the holiday it would have been a disaster, since besides the lovely Bay there wasn't a lot going for it. There was an evening show somewhere at the end of the Promenade, but it was not suitable for the children. Besides that there was very little entertainment, except for a sideshow standing about half way along the Front, the type found at funfairs where you have to throw three wooden balls into a bucket to win a prize. We all had a go but Sally seemed to have a real knack for it, and by her second "go" she had won a prize, then she had another "go" and won another prize. After about four "goes" and four prizes, the stall owner was looking a bit sick.

"That's enough for me," said Sally, not wanting to wear out her welcome. The owner gave her a big smile (and a big sigh), making a big presentation of giving her the final prize — which in turn attracted more people to his stall.

Every day, after that, when he saw us walking towards him he would cry:

"OH NO — LADIES AND GENTLEMEN — HERE IS THE LADY WHO IS DETERMINED TO RUIN ME!"

Sally felt embarrassed when everybody around looked at her, and at first wasn't going to play the game again, but at the owner's insistence and encouragement she felt almost obliged to throw the balls. It turned out to be more like a demonstration to show how easy it was, which the owner capitalised on and challenged other bystanders to try their luck. As far as we could see, though, it was only Sally who had the knack and she was the only one who ever won anything.

Another day I asked Sally and the girls if they would like to go out in a rowing boat for a change and they agreed. What we hadn't realised was the tide was still going out when I started rowing. So, in the beginning, when I was rowing out to sea, I thought I was making amazing progress, but when Sally said she thought we had better head back to shore and I turned the boat around, I realised that the tide had other ideas. As I struggled to make any headway, Sally commented something about how she hoped we weren't all going to be swept out to sea, and suddenly Jill and Joan went wide-eyed and very quiet.

It was another two hours before the tide turned and another half hour after that I appeared to be making some progress back to the jetty. When we eventually stepped on dry land again, with shoulders aching as if I had dug an acre of ground by hand, I vowed that would be the last time I would take a rowing boat out on the sea. In future a river or lake was a better idea!

"Good job we didn't take the boat out at Weston-Super-Mare," said Sally, later. "I can just imagine what the newspapers would have said: TERRIFIED FAMILY ADRIFT IN ATLANTIC. "

The following year we went to Bournemouth and loved the place so much that we went there for quite a few years after that. We always stayed at the same hotel situated not far from the cliff lift. There was a lot more to do at Bournemouth and one of the main attractions for Jill, besides the big breakers which rolled onto the beaches, was the Ice Skating Rink and the wonderful Ice Shows usually held there.

About the second time we stayed at the same hotel we met another couple at mealtimes. Their names were Joe and Lilian and they came from Wigan. We soon found we all got on very well and over the following years we would arrange to spend our holidays together in Bournemouth. They had both been married before and each had lost their partners in the war. Joe's wife had lost her life in the London Blitz and Lilian's first husband had been shot down over Germany. Joe hadn't come through the War unscathed, either. He had an artificial arm, which he said he'd had a bit of fun with, at dances, in the past.

"Depends how much I'd had to drink," he laughed. "And how many of my mates egged me on."

We had noticed that his arm appeared to be a bit stiff but hadn't realised the extent of his disability until he pointed it out.

"I always wore leather gloves when I went dancing and I would secretly detach the prosthesis before the end of the dance. When the music stopped I would thank the girl and walk away - leaving her holding it!"

When Jill was about sixteen or seventeen and wanted to go on holidays with her friend, Sally and I decided to go abroad. We weren't too adventurous the first year, just more or less tiptoeing across the channel to Ostend in Belgium, where we found a lovely Pension on the sea front. I practiced my smattering of French when required and we enjoyed it so much that we returned to the same place the next year.

Once Sally had a taste of "going abroad" she was eager to further the experience. As for me I was enjoying it too, feeling different from when I had returned from the war and vowed I never wanted to leave England again unless under duress. Now going overseas was very appealing and we decided before we could travel even further we needed a car. With a car our options would open wide, we decided. So we began to save in earnest.

CHAPTER THIRTEEN

The Day Wally went Daffodilling

We were just about to have our Sunday dinner when the front door opened and I heard my brother Wally calling up the hallway. The next minute he was sitting on the seat just inside our living room. By his side was his young son, Trevor, aged about three or four years, holding a small bunch of daffodils in his hands.

"Someone's been busy," I said, and Trevor smiled shyly, offering half of the flowers to Sally, who took a great delight in the gift, immediately thanking him and putting them in a vase of water, placing them in a prominent position on our sideboard. I thought Wally was looking unusually pale and when he pulled out a handkerchief to mop his brow I noticed that he was sweating. There were other different things about him, too. Usually his clothes were neat and tidy; now they looked just the opposite, generally dishevelled and grass-stained. He even had a couple of leaves stuck in his hair.

"What the hell happened to you?" I said.

"You'd be the same if you'd been where I've been," he said.

It was clear now that he was in some kind of shock and I quickly found the bottle of whiskey in the back of the cupboard and poured him a glass.

He drank it down. "I needed that," he said, leaning back in his chair.

I poured him a second drink, but this one remained in his hand until he had finished his story.

"As you already know, our Trevor loves flowers," he said.

Trevor beamed and nodded, confirming Wally's statement.

"So when he saw some kids coming home with bunches of daffodils tied to the handlebars of their bikes the other day, he asked me if we could go and get some too. I didn't want to ride all the way to Newent. That would be too far with him on the back of the bike, and I thought there might be some flowers around Sandhurst if we were lucky, so I told him we could go and have a look to see what we could find. He was really pleased at the thought of it."

Trevor nodded and smiled as he nibbled a biscuit that Sally had given him.

"I must have peddled for bloody miles and never saw a single flower," said Wally. "Then just at the point when I wanted to head for home Trevor spotted some daffodils in a field. 'Pleeease, Dad,' he said. By this time I was worn out and tried to put him off, but he was having none of it. He really wanted them."

Trevor nodded, verifying the truth of the story.

"So I stopped and told him to sit on the top of the five-bar gate that led into the field and wait for me whilst I picked the flowers on my own. That was the quickest way, I thought, otherwise we'd be at least another hour and we'd never get home. The flowers were about a third of the way across this field diagonally to the left and I decided to walk to the furthest point and pick them as I slowly walked back towards Trevor. That way I could keep my eye on him. Anyway, I had only just started picking some when Trevor yells out 'Dad!' I didn't take any notice at first because I thought he might have seen some more flowers and I wasn't interested at that point. The ones I was picking would have to be enough, I thought.

" 'Dad!' he yelled again, and I shouted back to him to be quiet and that I was picking the flowers as quickly as I could and would be back with him in a few minutes. But he wouldn't shut up."

Trevor's little face looked serious now as he relived the moment.

" 'Dad, Dad!' he yelled.

" 'WHAT IS IT?' I yelled back — really exasperated by this time.

" 'There's a big black bull behind you.'

"I turned around and saw this enormous animal heading straight for me. I nearly died, and as I began to walk quickly towards Trevor, it started running. So I ran — and it ran faster. I looked back again and it was gaining on me. Suddenly I knew I wouldn't reach the gate before he got me, so I did the only thing possible and took a flying leap over the big hedge, and landed in the ditch on the other side. And — you'll never believe this — but as I lay there — winded — the bloody thing was breathing and snorting through the hedge at me!"

"So Trevor saved your life!" said Sally.

"He certainly did!" said Wally, proudly putting his arm around his small son.

Trevor smiled shyly and nodded in confirmation.

CHAPTER FOURTEEN

Careless Talk

About three years after the war I was working with the Ministry of Works as a stoker and had been sent to the Brockworth Hostel site after an earlier familiarisation of the work at Robinswood Hill Barracks. The Hostel had been built to house workers during World War II and was still used by workers employed at the local factories and offices. There was a small cinema that opened Tuesday and Sunday evenings, and dances were held in the large Community Hall on Saturday evenings.

To my amazement, the first person I saw when I entered the Boiler Room that first day was Charlie Jones, still with a cigarette in the corner of his mouth, just as I remembered him. He wasn't a tall man, but he had a strong, solid build. His hair had thinned slightly and gone a bit greyer, but otherwise he looked the same as when I first met him in the Lounge Bar of the Northgate Hotel, just after the war had ended. We were both still on demob leave. Charlie had served with the Worcesters. Like many other returned servicemen, he felt undecided what to do back in civilian life — which direction to go — after the previous years of upheaval

105

and all decisions being made for you. He told me that he'd been a butcher/slaughterman in Worcester before the war, but now he didn't want to go back to the same job again, not on a permanent basis anyway. He said that he was living with his wife and two daughters at Brockworth, on the outskirts of Gloucester.

"Well, look who it is," I said, pleased to renew the acquaintance after all this time. "How long have you been here?"

"Oh, it must be getting on two years," Charlie said, smiling, and we shook hands.

"So you didn't go back to your old trade after all," I said.

"No, but I have kept my licence, and I've been doing a bit of slaughtering on the local farms when required. Only bacon pigs, and sometimes I do the curing as well. It's been a good little earner. Of course, the farmer must have the correct authorisation form from the appropriate Government Department."

Providing the animal was for home consumption and not for sale, it wasn't necessary to take your pig to a slaughterhouse for killing. However, a licence had to be obtained from the Ministry of Food each time a pig was slaughtered, and only one licence would be issued at any one time. In other words the Government would not let a farmer slaughter more than one pig for himself while there was still a food shortage in the country.

I told him about my pigs and how a slaughterhouse had killed one of them for me, before passing it on to a local butcher to do the curing. It had turned out to be a long-winded affair. So when Charlie offered to kill and cure one for me whenever I needed, I was pleased.

I hadn't been at Brockworth long when Charlie asked me if I would help him with his slaughtering that weekend. He said he had two farms to go to, adding that he would see that I was looked after "so don't forget to bring a bucket". I willingly agreed. We seemed to work well together and a bit of extra money would go towards our savings for a car, I thought. There was no doubt about it, Charlie knew his job well and the weekend went like a breeze, turning out to be the beginning of a lasting friendship and a good working relationship in both our working areas.

That first weekend I returned home with a full bucket. Most farmers didn't bother with the livers and chitterlings (the pigs' intestines), so we had those plus a small piece of meat each — always the cheaper cut. The chitterlings were a very popular dish amongst the working class and I took my share home, with relish. I would sit in the shed at the bottom of the garden, painstakingly turning them inside out with a stick to thoroughly clean them. Then they would be placed in a big enamel bath and covered with salt water. During the next twenty-four hours the water would be changed four or five times. Eventually, after all that, I would plait them together and then boil them until they were tender.

One day while we were working at Brockworth, a local farmer named Scrivens drove into the works yard and asked for Charlie. He wanted him to kill and cure a bacon pig for him, he said. It appeared that he had all the necessary papers, and arrangements were made for the job to be carried out the following afternoon, after we finished our normal day shift at three o'clock. By the time Charlie and I arrived at the farm the following day it was nearly half past three and we found the farmer already waiting for us. We were led to a large pen containing two pigs, each weighing about two hundred and forty pounds. One was a Large White, while the other was a Landrace pig. Both were fine looking animals.

"Which one do you want slaughtered?" Charlie asked the farmer.

"They're both about the same weight. I don't think it really matters," he replied. Then after a quick think, he said: "OK, make it the Landrace. When you've finished you'll find me in the milking shed."

About two hours later when our work was complete, Charlie fetched the owner over to show him where we had hung the carcass. Mr. Scrivens stood looking at it for a minute, as if he was deciding his next move — which as it turned out, he was.

"What about the other one?" he said eventually.

Charlie said nothing. I looked from one to the other, curious to see what was going to happen next.

"I'll make it worth your while — there's another five quid in it for you plus the extras, of course." As an added incentive he added: "No one would know."

Charlie turned away and rubbed his chin. It was clear he was giving the whole idea some serious thought.

"OK," he said, eventually. "But not one word to anyone, not even your missus, because this could cost me my licence!"

The farmer beamed with delight. "Don't worry, Charlie, my word on it! When you've finished the job and are ready to leave, give me a shout." With that he was gone again.

It must have been about six thirty by the time we hung the second carcass next to the first one and put the bonus meat into our respective buckets in the back of Charlie's car. Then I went to fetch the farmer. He was very pleased with the job and immediately settled the account with Charlie. Arrangements were made for the curing to take place the next day.

"You've done a good job," he said, with a broad smile. "Come on, we'll go and have a pint before you go home — reckon you've both earned it. Go on down to the Vic and I'll follow in my van."

The Vic was the name of the local pub and the thought of a refreshing beer after our hard day's work sounded like a good idea. So Charlie and I headed off to the pub and not long afterwards the farmer joined us in the Public Bar.

"Come on through to the Lounge Bar," the farmer said. "It's much more comfortable in there — the seating's better for a start." We followed him through to the adjoining room where we relaxed and sipped our cool beers — at least Charlie and I did. The farmer turned out to be a whiskey drinker, and a talkative one at that, as we soon found out. What had started out as a pleasant social drink with friends after a hard day's work soon turned into a very worrying situation. There was only one way to describe Mr. Scrivens — he was a "loose cannon".

"They don't know it all — eh, Charlie?" the farmer said, chuckling to himself, followed by various other obvious hints. As the farmer's voice got louder and louder, Charlie's face grew darker and darker. Then a few minutes later after finishing his umpteenth glass of whiskey, and giving us a knowing wink, he said: "There's nothing to beat a bacon sandwich, eh, Charlie?"

That did it — I could see that Charlie had reached the limit of his patience, and he suddenly stood up. A thought flashed through my mind. I wondered if they had ever had a fight in the Vic's Lounge before. But I didn't have to worry — Charlie was a lot more controlled than I would have been.

"Well," he said, "I think we'll make for home. See you tomorrow afternoon," and we made a quick departure, leaving the farmer with a surprised look on his face.

Once we were in his car Charlie really let loose.

"That's the last time I'll kill anything for that big-mouthed sod. Everybody could hear him in that Lounge!"

He was right — nobody could have helped hearing.

"Forget it, mate," I said, trying to calm him down, although my sympathies were with him. "Get the curing over tomorrow, and you can forget all about it. Live and learn. Come on, you've got to take me home, unless you want me to carry those buckets in the back of the car for about four miles." The image of me struggling along a country lane with a bucket of chitterlings suddenly struck us as funny and we both burst out laughing.

"You're right," Charlie said. "He's not worth thinking about!"

At about eleven the next morning the farmer drove into our works yard. One look at him told us something was drastically wrong. He looked pale and sick, with a hint of trembling about him.

"Where's Charlie?" he asked anxiously.

"Hang about — I'll find him for you," I said, leaving the farmer holding on to the door of his car, and quickly located my friend in the garage not far away. He was doubled up, checking the pressure in his tyres.

"There's somebody 'ere to see you," I said.

"Who's that?" he asked.

" 'Big Mouth'," I said. "He's waiting by his car in the yard."

Charlie let out a sigh, straightened up and rubbed his forehead with the back of his hand; it was obvious the less he saw of the farmer the happier he would be. "What the hell does he want now?" he asked as he cleaned his hands on a rag and walked outside.

The farmer walked quickly towards us.

"What's up?" asked Charlie.

"I've had a couple of inspectors from the Ministry of Food up to my place," said the frightened farmer. "They said they were going round the area, and according to their information I had been issued a licence to slaughter a pig. I told them that was correct.

Then one of the blokes asked me if I would be kind enough to show them the carcass. Honest, Charlie, I nearly died. I knew the two carcasses were hung together in the shed and there was nothing I could do about it. When they saw the two carcasses, the one bloke said, 'According to our books you had a licence for only one pig. What about the other one?' I was speechless — what could I say? Then the second bloke said: 'There's something seriously wrong here and we will have to remove both carcasses. We will issue you with a receipt for them and we must warn you that proceedings may be taken against you for exceeding your limit.' With that he gave me a receipt — here it is — and they took both the carcasses away in a van."

"Did you ask them for any identification?" asked Charlie, as he looked at the receipt.

"No," replied the farmer, "I was that bloody scared, my mind went blank."

"It must have done, if you accepted this as genuine!"

I looked over his shoulder at the receipt in his hand. It was just a plain piece of paper pulled from an ordinary notebook. On it was written: "Received from Mr. Scrivens, two pig carcases on behalf of the Ministry of Food, (signed) John Smith".

"John Smith?" I laughed at the universal anonymous name and the paper — there was nothing official looking about it. How could the farmer have been so stupid?

"What can I do?" he asked, suddenly realising he had been duped.

112

Charlie smiled, thoughtfully. "Well, you could go to the police, or you could get in touch with the Ministry of Food."

"I can't do that, because there were two carcasses instead of one."

"I know that and you know that," said Charlie. "AND the fellows who took your pigs know that. I'll bet you anything those two blokes were in the Lounge Bar last night, listening to you when you were spreading your good words about. They put two and two together and came up with four — the jackpot. Now you've been conned and as far as I can see there's not much you can do about it. You should have kept your big mouth shut."

As I watched the farmer walk slowly back to his car and drive away, I couldn't help feeling sorry for him.

"Poor bugger," I said. "He's lost two pigs, plus the fifteen pounds he paid us — and no bacon sandwiches."

"What are you on about?" cried Charlie. "Don't be sorry for him, it was his own fault. I could have lost my licence over his careless talk."

CHAPTER
FIFTEEN

My Father Dies

I had just finished the morning shift and was sitting in the living room at home with a much needed cup of tea, anticipating a leisurely look at the newspaper, when there was a knock on the front door and on answering it I found a young boy aged about ten years.

"I've bin asked to give yer this," he said, handing me a folded piece of paper, before disappearing off down the road on his bike. I opened it and found a hastily written note from my sister Lil, saying that our father had been taken into Great Western Hospital. I knew he hadn't been well for a while and nobody seemed to know exactly what the problem was, but the thought that it was serious enough for him to be hospitalised had never entered my head.

I grabbed my bike and rushed straight over the Horton Road crossing and down Great Western Road to the hospital, where I checked at the office situated at the main entrance for the location of his ward. After five minutes of numerous corridors and covered walkways I located it. The Sister in charge was sitting at a desk in a small glass-partitioned office just inside the entrance to the ward, from where she had a full view of the ward and anyone entering or leaving. I quickly introduced myself and asked how my father was.

"He's a very sick man, Mr. Lawrence," she said. "And I must warn you that he can go at any time." The news came as a bit of a shock.

"Go at any time?" I repeated, hardly able to comprehend. Surely not my father — tough as boots — indestructible.

"Does 'e know that?" I asked.

"No."

"What's wrong with 'im, then?"

"It's his heart — the valves have caused the problem," she said, and went on to explain in more detail, giving me the medical name of the condition. It was the last thing I expected. He was only 62 years of age and too young to die. I'd have expected his liver to fail before anything else judging from his favourite pastime.

I looked through the windows into the ward and could see Dad in his bed about half way along, his head leaning back against his pillow. Then he turned his head and I could see his face, white and gaunt. He spotted me and waved, and I walked along to his bed.

"What did 'er 'ave to say about me, then?" he asked when I reached him.

"She said you're going along fine." I sat down in a chair next to his bed. Putting on a brave face wasn't easy. I had always felt a strong bond with my father. The trouble was that I hadn't felt that my feelings were reciprocated and therefore had hardened myself over the years against the hurt. Now, seeing him lying there, it was hard to believe that he was so close to death and we had spent such little time together over the years. All those missed opportunities. Could the doctors be wrong? Miracles did happen — the papers were always writing about someone making a miraculous recovery somewhere in the world. Perhaps if he pulled through we could make up for lost time.

"I've been thinking," I said. "When you get out of this place, why don't I take you on a 'oliday somewhere — just you and me?"

"Oh aah," he smiled in agreement. "That 'ud be nice."

"The main thing is you've got to 'urry up and get well."

"Don't you worry, I'll be out of this place in no time. Where did you fancy going?"

"It's up to you," I said.

"I always liked Weston-on-the-mud," he laughed. "And that's not too far away."

"That's all right, then. Weston it is!"

We went on talking about a few things in general, and rugby in detail, until he became tired.

"Well, I better be off," I said.

"See yer tomorrow, then," he smiled and weakly lifted his hand in a farewell gesture. "And don't forget, I'm going to keep yer to that 'oliday when I get out!"

I laughed and was about halfway out of the ward when he called me back.

"Try and make it a bit earlier tomorrow," he said.

"Tell yer what — I'll come straight from work!"

"That's good," he said, and I left.

Unfortunately things didn't work out as planned. The next day there was a cloudburst just as I left work, and I got soaked through to my skin. There was no alternative other than to race home and change, so by the time I reached the hospital it was about half an hour later than my intended arrival. Then as I reached the entrance to the ward I was met by my sister Lil, and stepsister Doreen, both crying their eyes out.

"What's up?" I asked, concerned to see them in such a state, and knowing that something awful had happened.

"'e's just gone . . ." Lil said, tears streaming down her face.

"It was real sudden, Bill," said Doreen. "One minute 'e was talking to us — and then 'e was gone." She crumbled into sobs again.

I couldn't believe it and pushed past them to his bed. He was lying there with his glasses still on and his eyes were wide open, as if he was staring at something on the far wall. My fingers went to his temples and then to his neck. I was sure I felt a faint pulse somewhere.

"Nurse, nurse, quick!" I called out. "My father's still alive!"

But she was already at my side, checking him.

"No, I'm sorry, Mr. Lawrence," she said kindly, "but he isn't." She leant over to remove his glasses and close his eyes and I realised she was telling the truth.

His mother had been the same age when she died.

Later, when I thought of my father, I wondered why he had asked me to be earlier the next day. Did he, somehow, have a premonition of his own death?

Had Fate stepped in with the cloudburst to stop me being there on time?

Not knowing the answers made me cry even more.

Several months later tragedy struck again. It was 5.15p.m. on a Monday teatime and Sally's father and I were at home. He had just returned from the allotments and was busy laying the fire while I was in the kitchen helping to prepare the evening meal, which I often did if I was home before Sally. She had recently been made the manageress of Quality Cleaners, a dry cleaning shop in Barton Street, after working for a couple of years as an assistant in the company's shop in Westgate Street. Jill was at her elocution lesson with Marjorie Miles in Stroud Road and was due home about 5.20 pm. After her lesson she would always call in to see her mother at work to say hello, before continuing home.

I made a pot of tea and put it on the table and returned to the kitchen and not long afterwards could hear the fire crackling.

"Our Jill should be 'ome any minute," Dad said.

"Is it that time already?" I said, popping my head round the corner again to check the clock on the mantelpiece before continuing with my work.

Then there was a noise of some kind and I thought he had spoken to me.

"What's that?" I asked, but there was no reply.

Putting my head round the corner to ask again, I was shocked to find him slumped in his chair. I moved round the table and touched his shoulder and spoke to him, but there was no response. On further checking there was no sign of a pulse, either. I looked at the clock. Jill was going to be home at any minute and the last thing I wanted was for her to find her grandfather like this. So I raced to the front door and looked along the street. She was nowhere in sight. Next I ran over to Dan Cove in the fish and chip shop opposite, told him what had happened, and asked him to call for a doctor. At the same time I asked if he could look out for Jill and stop her from coming over to our house until I let him know.

Then I went back in the house and lifted Dad over my shoulder and carried him upstairs. He was a much smaller man than Mr. Smith, the hairdresser, who had lived opposite and who had needed a rugby scrum of local housewives besides myself to get him up his stairs. Our house was half the size of that house, with a smaller, narrower staircase and it still turned out to be a very difficult job. Nevertheless I managed it and laid him out peacefully on his bed, leaving me shocked and completely exhausted at the end of it.

The next minute Sally was dashing in through the front door, already on the verge of tears, anticipating the bad news. She was on her own.

"What's wrong? Dan just told me I should come in alone."

"Where's Jill?" I asked.

"She's staying over there."

"It's yer Dad," I said and took Sally upstairs to see him. Then the doctor arrived and confirmed that Dad had died.

Sally wrote a note for Jill to deliver to Mrs. Redfern who lived in a street off Derby Road. She was the local "layer outer", the person everyone called when someone needed to be "laid out" after death, in preparation for burial. Within the hour she arrived with her large black bag, saying how sorry she was to hear of our loss, and disappeared upstairs with bowls of hot water and towels to perform her duties. When she was ready to leave, Sally paid her the seven shillings and sixpence which was the set fee, and as Mrs. Redfern took the money she gently squeezed Sally's hand and whispered: "Your father was a very clean man," as if in some way the words might ease her grief.

Later, I asked Jill why she hadn't been home at the usual time.

"That was my fault," said Sally. "For some reason I told her to wait for me and we would walk home together."

"But she always comes home before you. She's never waited for you before," I said.

"I know," said Sally. "I don't know what happened. Jill was already to leave when I suddenly decided to make her wait. Don't ask me why, because I couldn't tell you."

Had Fate shown its hand again, I wondered?

CHAPTER
SIXTEEN

Paddy

While I was still working as a stoker for the Ministry of Works at Brockworth Hostel I met a bloke named Eric Wasley. Not to be confused with another Mr. Wasley who collected our Insurance money each week — a man who, like Eric, had many stories to tell. One in particular has remained firmly in my memory. It was the time he ran into the sea at Swanage in his new parachute silk swimming trunks, completely oblivious that the lining was missing and that without it they would become shockingly transparent once they were wet. He said that when he came out of the water half the people on the beach laughed, whilst the other half shrieked with horror. This turn of events devastated and embarrassed him dreadfully, but luckily, when he realised what had happened, he had the presence of mind to grab the hanky off his head and cover his face with it. He reasoned that way they wouldn't recognise him again.

The Eric Wasley at Brockworth Hostel was a likeable kind, who always seemed to be moving at double time, a perpetual motion sort of chap. I often wondered if someone wound him up every morning before he came to work. The strange thing was that for all the energy he expended during the day, he still remained slightly overweight. He had served in India with the Army during World War II and on occasions would fill me in, and anybody else within earshot, on some of his oriental experiences, relating his stories in his usual excitable manner, his mop of brown hair bobbing up and down as he gave emphasis to certain facts.

Eric was a fitter's mate to an Irish bloke we all knew — surprisingly enough — as Paddy, whose job it was to keep everything of a mechanical nature running smoothly. If something was beyond his capabilities, an outside contractor would be called in, but for most of the time he seemed to be competent enough.

Paddy was a bit of a mystery man. According to him, he had been invalided out of the Royal Marines before the war and at the start of the war had come over from Northern Ireland and found employment with the Ministry of Defence. Afterwards he was employed as the Fitter at the Hostel. This background didn't ring true to any of us, due to the many inconsistencies in the stories he would tell at different times. I had to admit, though, he looked the part with his solid build and confident manner. Aged about forty-five years of age with a swarthy complexion and black wavy hair beginning to turn to a steel grey, he would probably have remained a mystery man if a series of events hadn't unfolded to reveal otherwise.

Paddy lodged in the village with a widow named Mrs. Blackwell and her two daughters. After a while the elder daughter, Doreen, left home and took rooms in

Gloucester to be nearer her job, leaving Paddy with the widow and the younger daughter, Mary, who was now eighteen and working as a typist at a local factory. He had become genuinely fond of the widow and we half expected to hear the sound of wedding bells sometime in the not too distant future. Sadly, it wasn't long before the widow became seriously ill and within a few weeks died. Naturally Paddy and the daughters were totally devastated.

Time passed, and according to Paddy we were led to believe that the living arrangements at home were working out well, and that they were managing to cope with the household duties between them. This seemed hard to believe since he had always struck me as being on the chauvinistic side. For a start I could not imagine him ever washing up and was sure that Mary would be expected to do everything. No further mention was made of them until one Saturday morning about six months later, when Eric came into the boiler room, bursting with a good story to tell.

"Have you heard the latest?" he asked.

"What about?" I said.

"Paddy and Mary."

I shook my head. "What about them?" I said, putting my shovel against the wall.

"Well, it all started a week ago," answered Eric.

With a beginning like that I knew I was in for the long haul. "Grab a chair and I'll make some tea," I said. I had just finished stoking so was due for a break. Throwing a couple of spoonfuls of tea into the pot I filled it with boiling water. One good thing about

123

working with boilers, there was always plenty of it around.

"Well," said Eric, taking a mug of the hot brew from me and making himself comfortable. "Apparently when the widow died, and Paddy was left to share the house with young Mary, everything went well for a while like he said it did, but that was only until last Sunday — a week ago. They were having tea together when Paddy suddenly told Mary that he had two sons back in Ireland and that he thought it would be a good idea if they came to live with them because they couldn't find work at home."

"I didn't know he had any children," I said.

"Neither did I," continued Eric. "And neither did Mary from all accounts. It was the first time he had ever mentioned them. She hadn't even realized that he had been married. Anyway, he also suggested that she had better give up her job and keep house for them when they arrived."

"What a bloody nerve!" I said.

"Yes — and get this." Eric was really warming to the subject now. "When she asked why he hadn't said anything about it before, he said there was no point discussing the matter because he knew what was best, and besides, he had already made the arrangements for the boys to come over."

"So she had no say in the matter?" I said. "He had it all cut, dried and delivered."

"That's what I was told," said Eric.

"When are these two sons supposed to be arriving?"

"This morning at quarter to eleven!"

124

"This morning?" I looked at my watch it was already nine o'clock. "That's a bit short notice, isn't it?"

"He probably thought what he said would be law and his sons would be here within the week anyway so she wouldn't have time to think about it. But, as you can imagine, she was pretty cut up about it."

I bet she was, I thought. It would be bad enough being a dogsbody to someone who you weren't even related to, but then having to give up your job and wait on that person's sons as well — with less than a week's notice . . .

"What Paddy didn't know," continued Eric, "was that since her mother died, she'd been getting serious with a young bloke named Dave who also lives in the village. They'd been friends from school and it had developed into a love match. When Mary saw Dave that evening she told him about Paddy's plans and how she wasn't happy about her life being taken over. He'd already learned from Mary about Paddy's temper and now she said she was beginning to feel frightened. Not that he might touch her or anything like that — but because she knew he had a terrible temper and she feared things might get nasty if she didn't go along with his ideas. So they decided that something had to be done about it."

"I should bloody think so!" I said.

"Anyway," continued Eric, "Dave told Mary not to worry and they began to formulate a 'plan of action' so to speak. First, on the next day — Monday — they both got time off from work and visited the local council to confirm with them that the council house

125

that she was living in had been correctly transferred into the two sisters' names. The girls had done that after their mother's untimely death but Mary wanted to make sure. They both agreed to keep Paddy ignorant of how serious they were about each other or that she had even discussed the imminent arrival of his sons with him. As far as Paddy was concerned, Dave was an old school friend and that was all. After confirming the tenancy of the house, they went straight round to the Y.W.C.A. with the intention of moving Mary into the place straight away. That would leave Paddy to stew in his own juice, so to speak."

I quickly checked the gauges on the boilers and poured us both another cup of tea — this was beginning to sound like a thriller.

Eric took a sip and continued: "Stopping at the Y.W.C.A. was to be only a temporary measure because Dave had already secretly asked Mary to marry him and she'd agreed. So with the present circumstances forced upon them it made sense that they should make arrangements to marry as soon as convenient. In the meantime, however, they would keep it their secret."

"How come you know all this?" I asked, doubting that Eric had suddenly developed a sixth sense.

He pursed his lips and tapped the side of his nose in a knowing manner.

"Let's just say I've heard bits and pieces here and there." Eric was acting like an "investigative journalist" who did not want to divulge his source. He certainly had a way with a story and I was eager to hear the ending.

126

"So what happened next?" I said.

"Well, unfortunately when they got to the Y.W.C.A. there wasn't a vacancy until today — Saturday."

"But today is the day that Paddy's sons are arriving."

"Exactly,"

"So what did Mary do?"

"There was nothing Mary could do but stay in the house until this morning, then while Paddy went to meet his relations, Dave planned to pick up Mary and deliver her to the Y.W.C.A."

"And when he arrived home with his family she would be gone and they'd have to get their own dinner!" I said, smiling at the thought of it.

"Yes," said Eric. "I'd love to see their faces. Anyway, once Mary's settled in to her new accommodation she's going to advise the council that she wishes to give a month's notice to quit the house."

I laughed out loud. "That's what you call 'pulling the rug from under him'. But having to stay in the house with Paddy until today would have been difficult."

"There was no alternative," said Eric. We sipped our tea for a minute, thinking about it. I checked my watch — it was ten o'clock. With any luck she would be in the Y.W.C.A. by now. At least we hoped so. There was nothing Eric or I could do about it. An hour ago I hadn't a care in the world and now I couldn't help worrying that everything would turn out all right for the young couple.

"Of course, after last night I don't know how it's all turned out," Eric said.

"What do you mean?"

"Well, it turns out that when Mary got home from work yesterday teatime, Paddy asked her if she had given in her notice to quit her job like he'd told her to. He said he hoped she had, because when his sons arrived today they would need looking after. Mary said, afterwards, that she doesn't know where she got the courage from, but she stood up from the table and, looking him straight in the eye, told him that she had no intention of giving in her notice for him or his sons or anybody else for that matter. And for his information she was leaving the house, permanently, herself — the same time that his sons would be arriving."

The girl was gaining my admiration by the minute. "What did Paddy say to that?" I asked.

Eric laughed. "Mary says that he nearly choked. Then he ranted and raved at her, saying that he had always said he would look after her and that was what he intended to do, whether she liked it or not. She was to give up her job like he told her, he said, and he didn't want to hear another word on the matter, but Mary was having none of it. She put her coat on and when Paddy demanded to know where she was going she told him to mind his own business, and if he tried to stop her she would scream the place down.

"After she walked out Paddy must have felt in need of something stronger than tea, because he turned up at the local a bit later and got in conversation with Mick Donovan. You know Mick — he wouldn't hurt a fly."

"Unless he wanted to sing," I said, laughing. Mick had a liking for exercising his vocal chords after a couple of drinks. It wouldn't have been so bad if he sang in tune.

"I saw Mick this morning and he told me all about it," said Eric. "Paddy was in a vile mood last night, he said, and was complaining about the slip of a girl who he was looking after and sharing a house with. Unwittingly, Mick told Paddy that he didn't know what he was talking about. Mary was a lovely girl, he said. He had seen her with her boyfriend, who had a reputation of being one of the best all round sportsmen in the district — as fine a fellow you would wish to meet."

"What sport does he play?" I asked.

"He's a black belt in judo for a start. That's besides playing cricket and football in the local teams."

I was impressed.

"Then," said Eric, "Mick told Paddy that he wouldn't be surprised if the young couple didn't get married soon so all his problems would be solved, which seemed to make Paddy even angrier."

"The only problem now," I said, "is what happened when Paddy got home last night, once he knew about Mary and Dave."

For once Eric didn't know the answer.

"Well, look at it this way," I said. "If anything really bad happened it would be all over the village." Eric nodded and drank down the rest of his tea, whilst I checked the gauges. The boilers needed attending and I picked up my shovel. Eric said he had work to do.

"Are you and Sally going to the dance tonight, Bill?" he asked.

"Definitely," I said. Sally and I loved dancing and the Hostel held regular dances. The band wasn't a big affair, just a quartet — but they made a lot of music.

"See you there, then," he said, and he was gone.

The dance was going well by the time Sally and I arrived and Eric was already sitting at a table with his wife. They waved to us to join them. I ordered some drinks at the bar. At the far end of it was Paddy with two young strangers by his side, who I took to be his sons. On his other side was Mick Donovan, already warming up with a spasmodic rendition of "Mother MacCree", much to the consternation of those close by. Paddy looked in a very sullen mood and I didn't think it was solely Mick's singing. Again I wondered if Mary was all right. I had only just returned to the table with the drinks when my questions were answered.

"Look, there's Mary with her boyfriend," said Eric, nodding in the direction of a young couple at the entrance.

"That's a relief," I said, and Eric nodded.

It was the first time I had seen Mary. She was a lovely looking girl with dark hair, and her pretty full-skirted blue dress made her noticeable amongst the crowd. Her partner, Dave, a strong, handsome young man in his early twenties, wore a dark grey suit. They made a handsome couple and were quickly greeted by a bunch of their friends. Everyone was soon admiring Mary's engagement ring and toasts were being made to the happy pair.

130

"I've heard that Dave's father is going to put a deposit down on one of the new houses being built on that new estate for a wedding present," said Eric.

It was amazing how Eric learned all these facts. He would have made a perfect spy. How could England have let such a worthy man slip through their fingers during the war, I thought?

I looked at Paddy back at the bar. He was watching the happy couple and from the look on his face was not pleased with what he saw. That's how the standoff remained for the whole evening, with Dave and Mary remaining with their friends in one part of the Dance Hall, whilst Paddy stewed with his sons and "Mick the singing Tormentor" in the adjoining bar — all in full view of each other.

It wasn't until the band was playing the Last Waltz that Paddy decided to make his move. He had been preparing himself for it all evening with liberal amounts of his favourite black drink, and just as the first chords were struck and Dave and Mary had taken to the dance floor, he wove his way through the other dancers to the happy couple.

"There she is with her 'fancy' man," he cried. A fine spray came from his mouth, and he wiped it away with his shirtsleeve. "Now I'm going to see what her grand boyfriend here is really made of!"

The other dancers quickly scattered at the onset of the confrontation, but Mary and Dave stood firm. Then Michael, who had been in the throes of telling Kathleen that he would take her home again, stopped singing as he heard Paddy's raised voice and he came staggering after his friend across the dance floor.

"Leave the girl alone," he said, attempting to grab Paddy's arm to pull him away but missing. "If it's trouble you're looking for, you'll be on your own." He made another attempt at Paddy's arm and this time caught his friend's jacket, but it was vigorously yanked away, causing him to lose his balance and he fell heavily, sliding a couple of yards across the polished floor, eventually coming to rest at the feet of a group of dancers. There was no stopping Paddy now as he glared at the couple.

"So you're the fine fellow that Mary has taken a shine to." He spat the words, attempting to goad Dave into striking him. "Well, I'm going to show you that no one makes Paddy McCarthy look like a fool, especially a slip of a girl. C'mon, why don't you show the girl how good you are and step outside?" He began to take his coat off.

What Paddy hadn't realized was that the local policeman, who was always around at the end of the evening to make sure the bar closed at the correct time, had witnessed his outburst and was already walking over to the three of them.

"We don't want any trouble, Officer," said Dave. "We just want to leave quietly, but this man has been threatening my fiancée and me."

"It's no good asking the police to help you — they won't always be around," said Paddy, staggering a little.

"Move along, sir, you've had enough for one night," the policeman said to Paddy, taking his arm and guiding him away towards the exit.

"Don't think you've heard the end of this," Paddy called back over his shoulder.

"And if we have any more of that, sir," said his escort, "I'll have to charge you with disorderly conduct."

Paddy's two sons were already waiting for him by the exit and they took an arm each and led their father away.

"I don't understand, Eric," I said. "Surely if Dave was a black belt in judo like you said, he would have gone outside with Paddy and taught him a lesson he wouldn't forget."

"No, Dave did the best thing. After all, Paddy had his two sons with him and besides that, if he had fought him outside, there would be a lot of witnesses, and the police would probably have to charge him with assault." Eric was right.

I thought that was the end of the matter and that both parties would go their separate ways, but on Monday morning Eric paid me another visit with the news that Paddy was in hospital, apparently the victim of a "hit and run".

"When did it happen, after the dance?" I asked.

"No, it was last night, Sunday, when he was on his own, walking down to the pub for a drink. Anyway, I'll go and see him tonight, after work, to see how he is," he said.

★   ★   ★

133

It was an excited Eric that greeted me the following morning.

"Have I got something to tell you, mate," he said.

"What's happened?"

"For starters, don't expect to see Paddy again in a hurry."

"Blimey, he hasn't died has he?"

"No, but he probably wishes he had!" laughed Eric. "It turns out that our Paddy isn't all that he made himself out to be after all."

"Did they get the vehicle that knocked him down?" I asked.

"No. It was the police who thought it was a 'hit and run' but Paddy said it wasn't — and he wouldn't say any more on the matter."

"It must have been something hard that hit him, to have been mistaken for a 'hit and run' accident," I suggested.

"Mmm," said Eric.

"Do you mean it was something to do with a black belt?" I asked.

"Wouldn't be surprised — I reckon it was. That's what the locals are saying, anyway."

"So Dave did teach him a lesson after all," I said.

"Yes, it looks like it," said Eric. "And if Paddy did decide to lay charges for assault against Dave, who would believe that he didn't start it himself? Too many people witnessed his outburst at the dance on Saturday, and Dave's refusal to fight him."

"That's right," I said. "When is he coming back to work?"

"He was already gone when I got to the hospital."

"That's odd," I said.

"So I went home and who should be there but Dave and Mary."

"Dave and Mary?"

"Yes, they're good friends of our kid — my younger brother who lives with us. They want him to be their best man at their wedding."

"Now I get the picture," I said. "That's how you knew about everything that was going on!"

Eric laughed. "Oh, and there's one other thing — it appears that in the next bed to Paddy while he was in hospital was a bloke who had been in the 'Red Caps' attached to the same regiment as Paddy, during the war. He recognised him as a deserter who had been on draft for overseas duty in 1943. The bloke said that he thought there was something familiar about Paddy from the moment he set eyes on him. Then he remembered that the deserter in question had a tattoo on his upper left arm, in the shape of a heart with a dagger through it with 'Ireland for ever' written around it. The police checked, and sure enough, there it was.

"After further investigation it was verified that Paddy was, in fact, Shaun Murphy who had deserted and who it was thought had gone over the border to the Republic of Ireland. Earlier yesterday, before I got to the hospital, the Military Police took Paddy into custody. So it looks like that's the last we'll be seeing of him."

"I'll tell you one thing, Eric," I laughed. "You can certainly tell a good story."

★ ★ ★

Shaun Murphy alias Paddy McCarthy was taken into custody by the Military Police and later given a dishonourable discharge. His two sons vanished from the scene and it was revealed later that one of them had, in fact, been his nephew whilst the other was a cousin. Doreen Blackwell gave up her flat in town and returned to the family home with Mary. Later, Dave and Mary were married and moved into their new house.

CHAPTER
SEVENTEEN

The Sour Gooseberry Caper

Beyond the Tee Bridge were more railway allotments. Sally's father and I got one of them when he was alive and I kept it on after he died. It meant I had two allotments and a smallholding to look after, but I didn't mind because it meant I could grow all the fresh vegetables we needed besides the eggs and occasional rabbit. And any profits from the pigs went towards the car we were saving for. Besides Jill was about fourteen or fifteen by now and would often help feed the pigs and the other livestock if I wasn't able to make it.

I sometimes would pause when walking over the Tee Bridge to take in the view of the distant Cotswold Hills. With a picnic lunch we would often ride up to Painswick Beacon on our bikes, and sit with the sun on our faces and a hot flask of tea by our sides. When I say "ride up" it was more like "push up" beyond Upton St. Leonards. The Beacon wasn't much further in miles, but the time taken to push your bike up to it was possibly another half an hour. One consolation was that

137

we knew that we would freewheel almost all the way back into Gloucester on our return.

Such was the day when I paused, yet again, to take in the scenery and dream. Only this time, however, something down below caught my eye and distracted me from my thoughts, and when I looked I saw three teenage girls on my garden, about thirty yards away. Each was carrying a basket full of gooseberries — my gooseberries — from the look of it. Sour ones at that since they had not quite ripened yet. They must have felt they'd picked enough because the next thing they were walking along the path by the side of the allotments. If I called out to them they would definitely scarper, so I went for the more casual approach and remained where I was until I could see which way they were going to leave. They could either walk over the railway lines and make their way back down to the tunnel on the outside of the fenced pathway, which would have made it difficult for me to catch them, or they could be civilised and exit the allotments by a gate a short distance away on the other side of the Tee Bridge. To my relief they chose the latter, at which point I continued walking along the path towards them as if nothing was amiss until they were about to pass me, that is, when I suddenly grabbed hold of one of them by the arm.

"You'll do for starters!" I said.

The other two ran off, but not before I recognised one of the girls as the daughter of Mr. and Mrs. Jackson, who lived in Mill Street. The girl that I was still holding began to cry, so I grabbed the fruit from her and told her to go home.

"I'll be seeing you later," I shouted after her as she raced after her friends.

It didn't matter where she lived — the Mill Street address would be enough and first place to visit on my agenda after dropping the gooseberries home. Only Mrs. Jackson was home when I arrived at their house, and, when she heard what I had to say, she asked me if I would return that evening, about six thirty, when her husband would be home. I agreed.

When the appointed time came round for my second visit to the Jackson's house, my anger had subsided a bit. I'd been young myself and knew what it was like to pinch fruit when you're a kid. Often I had taken fruit from orchards when cycling in the countryside, but I didn't strip the trees! That was the difference here — they stripped the bushes bare — didn't leave one measly little gooseberry — not even ripe, either. Even so, I hoped that the father had already given his daughter a good reprimand over the whole incident, and the affair would be finished with.

I knocked on the brown front door of the house and Mr. Jackson, a slightly built man, opened it. He was holding the basket of stolen fruit and he handed it back to me.

"I'm very sorry, Mr. Lawrence," he said. "I've just given 'er a good talking to and I've sent 'er off to bed. You can keep the basket. 'er won't be needing it again!"

I thanked him, feeling pleased that the girl's father felt strongly enough about teaching his child the rights and wrongs of life, like Sally and I always did with Jill. Perhaps a lesson had been learned by at least one of the youngsters that day, I thought, and with any luck she would enlighten her friends. All my illusions were shattered in the next second, however, when his daughter Rosemary, the one who had stolen the gooseberries, came out of the house. Squeezing past her father on the doorstep, she sidestepped me and flounced off down the street.

Completely taken aback by it all, after what Mr. Jackson had just told me only seconds before, I looked back at him for his reaction, but he just half smiled and shrugged his shoulders, resignedly, as if he had no control over what his daughter did. Judging from what I had just witnessed and the fact that she was now dressed far beyond her years and looked more like an eighteen year old instead of a fifteen year old — it was the truth.

"That's bloody done it — I'm off to the police!" I said, my anger suddenly reignited. "Let's see what they've got to say about it!"

Rosemary gave a quick glance over her shoulder and hurried away even faster. At first, Mr. Jackson thought I was fooling around just to frighten the girl, but he soon realised I meant otherwise. Something had to be done to teach the girl a real lesson, for her own good, I thought, and if her father couldn't do it, I would.

The sergeant in charge at the local Police Station said he would get the other girls' addresses from Rosemary Johnson and in due course let me know any developments. The following day I had a visit from the Constable who was going to deal with the matter.

"I've already contacted the parents of the other two girls, Mr. Lawrence," he said. "And I might add that one of them became so irate when I told him the news about what his daughter had done that he had to be restrained from beating the girl."

I was shocked. "That's the last thing I want," I said.

"I thought that would be the case," he said. "You know, it would be a sad job if the three kids who are about to leave school ended up being summonsed."

I agreed that would be terrible and really didn't want to be too hard on them but it seemed that the message wasn't getting through to the girls without some drastic action.

"They seem to think that they can just help themselves," I said. "They don't realise that it's still stealing even if it's off somebody's allotment. Doubt if they'd steal from somebody's house but there's no difference is there?"

"That's right, Mr. Lawrence, there isn't. In this case, however, I suggest an official apology from them would be in order."

I savoured the idea for a moment; it sounded a good and just solution.

"How about I arrange it?" he said. I agreed and arrangements were made for the three girls to be at my home the following day at 5.30 pm.

At the appointed time there was a knock at the front door and Sally showed the three girls into the front room. She said later that she hadn't seen faces that white for a long time. I followed them into the room and found the three girls had squeezed themselves tightly together on the two-seater settee, which was quite a feat in itself since the settee was part of a cottage suite, a much more compact type of furniture suitable for small spaces like our front room, and was barely one and a half times the width of an ordinary armchair.

They looked very neatly turned out with faces looking so angelic that it was difficult to remain angry with them. There was no doubt about it, they had really tried to present a good image of themselves, and whether it was their "togetherness" or otherwise, I don't know, but the Gilbert and Sullivan song *Three little maids from school* came to mind. Then, as if it had all been rehearsed, which no doubt it had been, they apologized — in unison.

I thanked them and said that no action would be taken this time.

"But don't forget," I said. "The police have your names now, and if I catch you on the allotments again without a good reason, I'll definitely prosecute."

The girls nodded — again in unison — and rose as one from the settee.

Sally and I were glad to see that the colour had come back to their faces by the time they left. I never saw them anywhere near the allotments after that. Many years later there was an unexpected sequel to this story . . .

CHAPTER EIGHTEEN

The Car

After a few years I left Brockworth and worked as a stoker at the Record Offices in Eastern Avenue. The time saved in travelling to work was put to good use. Instead of the half an hour cycle ride to and from Brockworth each day, it was now a quick ride down the alley over the Tee Bridge, through the subway and home — all of ten minutes. And it was really handy for feeding my animals and doing a spot of gardening on the way.

I hadn't been working at my new job for very long when Jill left school and started looking round for a job. Whenever we had asked her what she wanted to do when she finished her schooling she would always say an actress or an artist, which seemed totally unrealistic to Sally and me, especially in a place like Gloucester.

I couldn't help blaming the elocution lessons and the couple of small parts in High School plays for putting the acting ideas into her head, but as for the art side of things we were at a loss where her talent came from. We had to admit, though, that she could draw and every spare bit of money would be spent on cartridge paper from the Barton Press. Years earlier, when Sally's father

143

had still been alive and Jill slept in the front room downstairs, her bedroom wall was covered with her work and anyone who visited us and showed any interest in art had been automatically invited into her room to view her permanent and ongoing exhibition.

She had always got As for Art in her school marks, but unfortunately her marks for other subjects never reached the same level, and it was clear that she would never reach the academic level required to study the subject at university. She did apply to Priestley's Studios in Gloucester with samples of her work, but there were no places available.

The other alternative was the Gloucester Art School, but that cost money, which we didn't have. Besides, as far as Sally and I felt, what good would it have been? I remember commenting to Jill at the time: "What's the point in learning about art? After all you can't earn any money from it." As far as we could see the only good artists were dead ones. (These words have often been quoted back to me over the years when she has sold her paintings.)

So, after several weeks of searching for employment and not being successful, I suggested that she apply to become a Civil Servant and train as a typist at Records. I had heard that they were taking applications and urged her to find out more about it. It was the last thing she ever wanted to do, but with nothing else in the offing we thought at least it would give her a practical skill that she could use throughout her life. In that respect it proved a good choice.

144

Within the month she applied and was subsequently accepted as a trainee and shortly afterwards she entered the Typing School to learn the skill of touch-typing. Several weeks later and now already resigned to her new occupation, she graduated from the school and subsequently moved into a typists' pool.

Meanwhile Sally and I had eventually saved enough money for our first car — a brand new one — and we took great delight in going to the showroom and picking it out. It didn't take long because we only had enough money for the cheapest in the range, the Ford Popular, but we didn't care. It was ours, it was new and we had paid cash. There was one problem, though; I still didn't have my driving licence. However, I was to sit it in a week's time and arrangements were made for me to pick it up immediately after I passed. Failing never entered my mind. Well — it did enter it a bit but I pushed it back out because I had studied the Road Manual thoroughly, and believed in "positive thinking".

A minute technicality was all it took — so minute that I can't even remember what it was — to fail the test. Afterwards I returned home extremely disappointed and had to arrange for the car to be delivered to me, instead. How could it have happened, I thought? Now our brand new car was parked opposite the Allington Hall outside the School in Derby Road, because we didn't have a garage, just waiting to be driven and me unable to oblige. That didn't stop us all going along and inspecting it.

Jill was disappointed when she saw it, though, saying it looked old fashioned. She had hoped it was going to be a later model, but Sally and I didn't care. The car was all new and shiny — and it belonged to us. We all climbed in the seats in turn, just to see what it was like, pleased with the roominess and the smell of new leather. Sally imagined the wonderful scenery she would see through her window and how many suitcases the boot would hold for holidays. In an attempt to console me Sally said that she had never heard about anyone passing the test the first time, but it made no difference. I felt cheated and another driving lesson and frequent visits to the car over the next couple of days, to check it out, didn't help.

On about the third day I walked along to where the car was parked and sat in it again. If I had passed my test, I thought, we'd have already done a couple of trips into the countryside by now. Perhaps even a run out to the White Hart at Sandhurst, where we would have a drink — just the one, like a responsible driver — and chat with the locals. Then when we were ready, we would all climb back into our new car and drive home again. After brooding over the situation for a while, I climbed out of the car and returned to the house.

"Bugger it — I'm taking it out!" I announced.

"What do you mean?" said Sally, obviously hoping she wasn't thinking what I was thinking.

"The car," I said again. "I'm taking it out!"

"Well, don't expect me to come with you when you haven't got your licence," said Sally. "You must want your head looked at, to even think about it!"

"That's a good one. Even my wife doesn't believe I can drive now," I said, trying to persuade her. "I keep telling you he failed me on a technicality."

Sally, in her wisdom, would not be swayed.

"Well, you get your licence first, then I'll come," she said, and carried on preparing a meal in the kitchen.

"They just want to get some more money out of me — that's what it's all about," I said, pleading my case. Jill was home from work by now and sitting in a chair listening to us.

"What about you, luv?" I said to her. "Do you feel like giving your father a bit of support?"

"You *can* drive, can't you, Dad?" she asked with doubt in her voice.

"Course I can!"

"Oh, all right, then," she said, jumping up.

Sally stood in the kitchen doorway. "I hope you realise what you're doing. You know you're breaking the law — and involving your own daughter too!"

"Nobody's going to see us," I said. "Anyway, who knows I haven't passed? I'm only going for a short ride. We shouldn't be more than about fifteen minutes."

With that Jill and I walked along to the car and the next thing I was driving over Horton Road Railway crossing, heading for Barnwood, where we turned into Upton Lane and then on to Upton St. Leonards.

Driving without a licence, I soon discovered, was pretty nerve-wracking stuff. If I got caught my driving days would be truly over — for a while anyway. So, when we reached Painswick Road, I pulled the car over to the grassy verge on the side of the road, stopped the

147

engine and pulled the brake on and relaxed for a minute.

"What's wrong?" asked Jill, thinking there was something wrong with the car.

"Nothing," I said, bluffing. "Just thought I'd have a practice at stopping and starting."

Deep down I felt satisfied that I had actually driven the car, but resolved that once the car was back home I would not drive it again until I had officially passed my test. The risks were too great. After a couple of minutes I started the engine again and attempted to release the break — but it wouldn't release. Again I tried, but it still remained locked on, firm as a rock.

"Just my luck," I thought, my mind racing. "All I need now is a policeman to pull up by my side and the next thing I'll be up in court with no chance of driving the car again for months, if not years."

I turned the engine off, and then started it again, following through the routine I had learned at my driving lessons, but it would not move. The light was gradually moving towards dusk and I realised that something had to be done soon. I told Jill that I would stop the next vehicle that came along and ask the driver to give her a lift to a garage further along Painswick Road. She would have to tell the mechanic what had happened and ask him if he could come back and help. A minute later I stopped a passing wholesale vegetable truck, which gave her a lift.

Meanwhile I sat and brooded about my predicament. Would the mechanic need to see my driving licence for any reason, I wondered? But when I couldn't think of a reason why he should, I dismissed that idea. The next worry was — what if there was something seriously wrong with the car and it had to go back to the manufacturers, would it still be under warranty? Then they would want to know what happened and everything would come to light. Why hadn't I listened to Sally? Then none of this would have happened.

I decided that whatever happened I would have to bluff my way out of it, and the next minute the garage truck was pulling up by the side of me and the mechanic and Jill got out.

"What's the trouble?" he asked, grabbing his toolbox from the back of his vehicle and walking over.

"Well, I started the engine and I couldn't release the brake," I said.

"That's strange," the mechanic replied climbing into the driver's seat. He grabbed hold of the brake stick, gave it a quick jerk — AND RELEASED IT. Then he looked at me as if I was crazy and said: "What's wrong with that?"

From where I was standing there was nothing wrong with it — it was perfect.

I tried to explain how the car was new — it was the first time I had driven it, and I hadn't realised that the break had to be jerked before releasing. He gave me a look of disbelief. Luckily I had enough money to pay for his "call out" before he drove off in disgust.

When Sally heard what had happened — there was no chance of keeping the whole episode quiet since the whole thing had been an adventure for Jill, and she was bursting to tell her mother all about it — she just looked at me and said: "Well, I hope you're satisfied!"

The next time I took my driving test, I passed it, much to everyone's relief. It had been torture seeing the car standing outside the school day after day, like a patient dog waiting for its exercise, and me no longer willing to oblige. I had learned my lesson, and it didn't help when a neighbour down the street, who was prone to standing on her doorstep for hours every day making a mental note of any movements in her vicinity, like someone working for Intelligence, "clocking them in and clocking them out" as Sally would say, stopped her as she was walking home from Quality Cleaners for lunch, a few days after my "brake ordeal", and put her through an interrogation.

"See your new car's still standing over there — nice, ennit?" the neighbour said.

"Yes," said Sally.

"'aven't seen yer out in it much, though, since yer got it. 'An't Bill got 'is licence yet?"

"No," said Sally.

"S'funny — I could 'ave sworn I saw 'im driving it the other afternoon. Your Jill was with 'im."

"Was she?" said Sally, making a quick getaway.

With the licence now safely in my pocket, we took the car for a run, and one of the first places I took it was down to my relations in Clapham. I hadn't told them that we were getting a car, wanting it to be a surprise. Aunt Else was serving a couple of customers when I arrived and I waited patiently till the shop was empty, anticipating her surprise and delight at what I had to show her.

"Come and see what I've got," I said.

"Oh, is it your new car? We 'eard you got one," she said, completely spoiling my day. How did she know? It turned out that Jill had mentioned it in the office where she worked and one of the girls working there was engaged to a relation. Who needs a newspaper when you've got a family grapevine?

CHAPTER
NINETEEN

The Flooded Cellar

My brother Wally was landlord of the Jockey Pub, opposite the Kingsholme Rugby Ground in Kingsholme Road. In fact a couple of the rooms at the back of the building were used for pre-match and post-match meetings by the rugby players. Sally and I would often go down to see Wally and his wife Rachel on a Saturday night and have a drink. It would always be late in the evening by the time we got there because it was a waste of time trying to get a word in edgeways with Wally before closing time. The place was always packed out and he would be too busy. After he closed the pub, however, it was a different matter and we would adjourn to his living quarters at the back of the pub with some of his other friends for a small party, often not leaving until the early hours of the morning. Before leaving home Sally and I would always go to bed for a couple of hours' sleep, otherwise we would never have lasted out.

There was one particular event that happened about this time, which Wally has often spoken of with much laughter — although at the time when it happened, he didn't think it was particularly funny.

One Saturday night when we arrived I noticed that he looked worn out and tired.

"What's up?" I asked him, when we were sitting in his lounge, afterwards. "I know you've been working hard all evening, but you look like you've just run the marathon."

"I feel like I have, too," he said. "It's the cellar — every time it rains the thing gets flooded and I've been baling it out with a bucket and a small foot pump, on and off, all day, and only more or less finished it just before we opened tonight. Thank God it's stopped raining, that's all I can say. It's a lot of work and I'm bloody fed up with it! Every time it rains it's the same thing, as if there isn't enough work to do running a pub."

Wally was never what you might call a big built bloke and the extra exercise had taken its toll.

"Is there nothing you can do to stop the flooding?" I asked.

"I'm working on it," he said. "In the meantime one of my regulars said that I should call the local Fire Brigade when it happens again, because it's their job to do things like that. They've got a pump that could do the job in no time. So that's what I plan to do next time."

It didn't rain for the next couple of days but on the following Friday it poured down again and my thoughts went to Wally and how he was managing. With the new plan of action he had mentioned the previous week I expected to see him looking more relaxed on the

Saturday evening. But he didn't. In fact he looked much worse and I told him so.

"That bloody cellar will be the death of me!" he said.

"Don't tell me you still had to bale it out again," I said. "What happened to the Fire Brigade?"

"The less said about that lot, the better," he said.

"What do you mean?"

"Well," said Wally, taking a sip of whiskey to fortify him in the telling of the cellar saga, "when it poured down yesterday and the cellar got flooded again, I thought I'd wait until this morning to assess the situation. When I had a look today it still looked pretty bad — easily as bad as last week, but I decided, just to be on the safe side, to make it look more worthwhile for them to pump out and added some extra water. I put the hose into the cellar and let the water run until it was about half the water again. Then I rang the Fire Brigade and told them I was flooded."

"So what happened?"

"When the Fire Engine arrived, the chief fireman walked into the pub holding a long measuring stick in his hand. I took him to the cellar and he stuck it into the water, read the measurement and said: 'I'm sorry, Mr. Lawrence, but this water is one inch below the regulated depth for us to pump — we can't touch it.' AND HE LEFT! "

CHAPTER
TWENTY

The Funeral Fiddle

After several years I returned to the same line of work as my first job after the war. At that time I'd hated it — now I loved it. Being older probably made all the difference. I had reached the age when obtaining a less physical job than stoking had became a priority and when an opportunity came along to work as a Security Officer again, I grabbed it with both hands.

The company I worked for had a large depot in India Road, and my base was a small office at the entrance to it. The office had all round vision and for most of the time our job was keeping an eye on the vehicles entering and leaving the premises, and their intended business. We were also expected to locate and apprehend any crooks in our midst, which for the most part was for petty theft such as small goods pilfering. An odd packet of polony smuggled out by a worker was taken for granted, being the nature of some people, but if an employee was actually caught with the goods they were given the sack. It never failed to amaze me, knowing the risks involved about losing their job, how certain people would push their luck to the limit in the belief they could get away with it. One such person in particular comes to mind.

It was to do with a sudden influx of pilfering in the small goods. The first we heard of this sudden food foray was when the foreman in charge of small goods came down to see me in the office. It was late November and no doubt the thieves were stocking up for the coming festive season — at the company's expense.

"The stuff's going left, right and centre," the small goods foreman said. "Will you see what you can do about it, Bill? The next 'big lift' will probably be on Thursday." He was sounding like Montgomery advising on troop movements.

"Why's that?" I asked.

"It's all the extra Christmas stuff we've got to get out. They're all on overtime at the moment. It'll be too much temptation for 'em, I reckon."

"Have you got any suspects?" I asked.

"There's one woman in particular," he said. "I've warned her a couple of times already about packing the stuff in her handbag before paying for it. She's the main one — must be taking enough stuff to feed a regiment." This bloke had to be in the territorials or something.

"What's her name?" I asked.

"It's Pat; I think she lives near you."

I suddenly realised who he meant. It was Pat who always called out "'morning, Bill" or "'night, Bill" when she passed the office. I knew her husband quite well and hoped the foreman's suspicions were wrong — unfortunately they weren't.

On the following Thursday I kept a special lookout for Pat when she came to clock off at the end of the day. And from the moment I saw her walking — or rather, waddling — towards me down the yard, the foreman's suspicions were confirmed. Normally a slight built woman, she now looked like she had suddenly gained a couple of stone since I had seen her that morning. She was on her own.

"'night, Bill," she said, as she put her card into the clock machine.

"Hang on, Pat," I said, getting out of my seat. "I want to see you."

She looked shocked, then turned her back on me for a second before turning back and taking a couple of steps away.

"No, wait, I won't keep you a minute," I said, stepping out of the office and walking round to where she was standing near the clock.

"Somethin' wrong?" she asked, her face attempting a look of innocence.

"What's all this, then, Pat?" I asked, pointing to the pile of small goods now scattered around her feet on the floor.

She looked down and, as if it was the first time she had seen the stuff, exclaimed: "Good God! Where did that lot come from? I must have nearly stepped on the lot. Surprising what some people'll get up to, ennit, Bill?"

"Well, it wasn't there a minute ago because I'd just walked through before you arrived," I said, which was the truth.

"Well, don't look at me!" she said, her face flushing.

"You know nothing about it, then?" I asked.

"What — me?" said Pat, suddenly stiffening her neck and pulling in her chin. "You should know me better than that!" It was a good show of righteous indignation and at the end of her performance she huffily turned round and left. I quietly picked up the food from the floor and returned to the office, without a doubt that she knew she was a marked woman. The following week she gave in her notice.

Months later there was another event, which showed just how devious some criminals could be. It all came about on a Saturday morning when I had returned to the office to pick up a book which I had left behind the night before after finishing my afternoon shift. I had a couple of days off and wanted to finish it off over the weekend. Another security policeman named Ken was on duty and I found him in a state of great agitation when I arrived.

"Am I pleased to see you," he said, when I entered the office. It was unusual to see him like this; he was usually a laid-back sort of person.

"What's happened?" I asked.

"There's a bloody fiddle going on — with petrol — in the Funeral Department."

Now I could understand why he was upset. It wasn't that he wasn't capable of sorting out any fiddle going on, but the fact it was to do with death. Ken had often mentioned to me his fear of it and even the thought of being in close proximity of a dead body filled him with horror. So everything to do with that department was

158

generally left for me to deal with. I didn't mind because it didn't bother me at all; I had no fear in that area, probably because I had worked as an undertaker's assistant when I was a teenager.

"How do you know there's a fiddle?" I asked.

"That's what the memo says." Ken handed me a piece of paper.

It was from Harry, the Funeral Services Executive Officer, Head of the Funeral Department, and read: "There have been discrepancies between the fuel usage and mileage regarding the funeral hearses over the past month. Would appreciate your investigation into the matter."

"Have they had any new blokes starting?" I asked. These sorts of fiddles could sometimes be connected to a new bloke joining the company.

"Yes, I already checked that out — he joined us a month ago. He's driving the hearse this morning. Him and another bloke from that department have gone to the hospital to pick up a body. I wouldn't be at all surprised if they only pinch the stuff when I'm on duty, because everybody knows I don't like being near bodies. It would be a different kettle of fish if you were here — they wouldn't try it then."

"Well, I'm here now, so stop worrying," I said.

I felt sorry for him. Everybody has a fear of something. Mine is shellfish, which makes me violently ill. Ken's was bodies — specifically, dead ones.

"They'll be calling in to refuel on the way back," he continued, "so they're ready for the next callout. I

159

reckon that's when they'll be getting the bit extra for themselves."

I had to agree. It would be easier for them to do it that way instead of syphoning it off later. All they had to do was fill some extra containers at the same time that they filled the hearse and stick them in the back of the vehicle and if they only did it when Ken was on, nobody would know any different. The bowsers were up the top of the yard a safe distance from the rest of the buildings and out of general view. It was a help-yourself system with just a logbook to fill out, with no-one to see where the fuel actually went.

"What am I going to do?" said Ken. "I won't be able to go near the box." The box was a metal container used to transport a body back to the Funeral Parlour before it was placed in a coffin.

"Don't worry," I said. "We'll give them a nice surprise. First, I'll go and move my bike so that nobody recognises it."

After putting my bike behind the building I returned to the office and decided my next move.

"I'll keep out of sight until they're about to leave," I said. "The empty garage half way up the yard should be a good spot. From there I can see the petrol bowsers and you. With any luck we'll catch them red-handed. Give me a wave when they're coming." With that I made my way across to my hiding place.

It wasn't long before Ken looked up towards me and waved. The next thing the hearse crawled through the gates and made its way past me, then it did a big circle at the top end of the yard and crept back to the bowsers where it stopped, facing down towards the gate. The new driver and his mate got out of the vehicle and walked towards the back of it and started refuelling, then the mate disappeared into the garage for a minute.

I was just about to dart back to the office when the mate returned to the back of the hearse and the new driver then walked across the yard towards the company office, opposite our security office. He was a tall, well-built bloke in his late twenties. It looked like he was delivering some papers, so I waited a minute. Meanwhile, back at the bowsers, the refuelling continued. Although it was out of my range of vision, I thought I could hear the back door of the hearse being opened and closed, but wasn't sure. After a couple of minutes the new driver walked back across the yard and rejoined his mate and they talked at the back of the vehicle for a minute before going into the garage. A minute later they walked a bit further up the yard, away from the bowsers, where they both lit up cigarettes and stood talking. At this point I made a dash for my office.

"Did they see you?" asked Ken.

"No," I said, pulling my chair round with its back to the windows and sitting low down in it. "When they come down to the gate, let me know. I won't show myself until then."

"Right," said Ken. "I'll stand outside where they can see me — but don't hang about. You know they'll expect to drive straight through like they usually do."

"Well, they're going to be disappointed, aren't they?" I said.

It was only a couple of minutes before Ken tapped on the window. The hearse had crawled to the gate and the driver was about to give his customary wave as he passed through, when I called out:

"Where are you going?"

"Oh," said the new driver. "We've just been up the hospital to pick up a body — it's in the back." He indicated the box. "We're taking it over to the Chapel of Rest."

"Well, let's have a look at it, then," I said.

"What do you mean?" he said. "What's going on?" He looked at his partner in the cab, but he just shrugged his shoulders.

"Nothing's going on," I said. "We're checking the vehicles this morning — just routine. Pull into that empty garage across the yard." I indicated the place I had been hiding shortly before. He did as I requested and when both men had climbed out of the vehicle, I did a quick search of the cab, but found nothing.

"Open the back — so I can see inside," I said.

The driver opened the door and I searched the interior. Again there was nothing — except for the box. I put my hand on it.

"You're not going to look in there, are you? That doesn't seem right," said the new bloke, looking quite shocked. "What are you looking for? There's only a body in there."

I ignored him and gently lifted the lid. Inside was the deceased — an elderly woman. Across her feet was a piece of white linen. I carefully lifted it and there, on either side of her feet, was a can of petrol. I stood back and looked at both of them. One thing I had learned all those years ago was to always handle bodies with respect and dignity. There appeared to be a complete lack of it in this case.

"What's going on here?" I said. "You haven't fetched that from the hospital!"

"Don't ask me," said the new bloke with a look of consternation on his face. "That's the first time I've seen it."

"Me too," said his partner. "It might be for the lawn mower over at the Chapel of Rest. I think the gardener needed some more fuel today." It was obvious he was making the story up as he went along.

"Come off it," I said. "If that's right, why can't he fetch his own fuel? Besides, what the hell is it doing in the box with the body?"

They didn't answer.

"Right, wait here," I said, leaving them to walk up the road to the Chapel of Rest, a short distance away, where I could see the gardener cutting the grass in the front of the building. If it was the gardener's fuel order, as it was suggested, why was it inside the box and not standing on the outside of it? Was it to stop it falling over in the back of the hearse and staining the panelling? I didn't think so! Anyway, nobody had mentioned that was the reason. Both the new driver and his mate denied any knowledge of it, and they were the only ones who could possibly have had anything to do with it. It had to be one of them and they both had the opportunity. Each man had been on his own at the bowser at some time during the refuelling.

The gardener stopped mowing when I approached.

"Have you ordered any petrol from the garage for your mowers today?" I asked.

"Yes, I've got it, thanks," he replied.

"You've got it?"

"Yes, I've got it — I fetched it this morning." He showed me the two cans. "As a matter of fact I've used nearly a full can already." He picked it up and shook it to prove the point. "Is there a problem?"

"Nothing for you to worry about," I said.

By the time I returned to the others, all three of them were looking pretty sick. I say three, because Ken was looking a bit pale round his gills as well. In his case, though, it was probably his being in close proximity to a dead body that caused it. I decided to have another go at the two funeral blokes.

"C'mon," I said. "Let's have the truth."

"Look, I don't know anything about the petrol or how it got there," said the new bloke.

"Nor me," said his mate.

"Well, you're not going anywhere yet — I'll ring the Funeral Department and get to the bottom of this!"

When I rang Harry, the Funeral Services Executive Officer, and told him what had happened, his first response was "Call the police!" That was the trouble with Harry; he never wanted to try and sort it out a bit himself, first. I wanted to try and nail the bloke at the bottom of it. Somehow, the new driver didn't seem the thieving type — I couldn't help thinking he was a bit thick. My instincts said it was his companion. In the end, though, I had to call the police since Harry had said so.

I knew the young detective from Barton Street Police Station and when he arrived I told him what had happened.

"All right, Bill," he said. "I'll take the new driver down with me first and have a chat with him, and see what we can find out."

About an hour later he was back.

"Well, there's a bit of a problem here, Bill. I think the new driver knows nothing about it and has been used, because he's very naïve. He's not short of cash, his wife works as a Sister in the hospital and they've got their own home. Before I do anything else, I'd rather you had a word with his boss yourself. Frankly, I think this bloke is innocent and the real culprit is his mate, but I haven't interviewed him yet. Look, we can go ahead and try and find out exactly what's been going on, but if it is the second bloke, and I think it is, and we do him, I'll have to do the new bloke as well, because he was the driver, and they both had opportunity! It seems a bit rough on him."

I called Harry and passed on what the detective had said and how the possibly innocent driver would be dragged into it all.

"Fair enough," said Harry. "Tell that detective we won't press charges — but both of them will have instant dismissal."

So that's what happened. I couldn't help feeling sorry for the new driver. He would have left the job wondering what it was all about but at least he didn't end up with a criminal record. Afterwards, when all the excitement was over and I was sat having a welcome cup of tea with Ken, I said, "Let's hope there's a new driver for the hearse on Monday morning in case they've got to pick up a body."

"Well, as long as they don't ask me to help out, I don't care," said Ken, giving another shudder.

CHAPTER
TWENTY-ONE

Spain

The summer after we'd bought the car was spent exploring far and wide. Sometimes, when I was off work for a weekend, I would pick Sally up from work at 5.30p.m. on Saturday evening, having already prepared and loaded enough food and drink to last overnight, and we would drive to Bournemouth, arriving later that evening. Then we would find a good spot in a car park in one of the cliff chines on the seafront, where we would sleep for a few hours until first light. It was a wonderful experience sitting and watching the dawn the following morning, while we sipped hot tea and ate our breakfast.

It wasn't long, though, before our sights were set further afield. Why not travel over to the Continent? We had liked Belgium a lot when we had explored that country, but now we had a car we could go somewhere a bit further away — somewhere that was still "untouched". Our interest began to drift towards Spain and the Costa Brava, which we had started to read about in the newspapers. Sally and I pored over the atlas and decided which route we would like to take and sent the information off to the Automobile Association. Within a short time we received a complete map already marked out for us with further bits of information we might require. It was as easy as that.

Our first trip overseas with the car was very exciting. Sally became the navigator and the journey went without a hitch — well, more or less. Before we started the journey we decided that wherever we were at 5.00p.m. each evening, we would find the closest accommodation, if we hadn't already booked in somewhere earlier that day. That way I could have a good rest before starting off early the next morning. This turned out to be a good move and over the following years we found some lovely, reasonably priced pensions hidden away in the countryside, where we could get clean accommodation and good meals.

Driving through France turned out to be a dream. The route we were given was easy to follow and didn't touch any of the large cities. My confidence grew by the hour and it wasn't until we saw the Pyrenees in the distance and how high they were, that it suddenly wavered. The thought crossed my mind — would the car make it? Being the cheapest car in the range also meant it had limited horsepower.

Slowly we crawled up the steep mountain road, with sometimes a sheer drop on one side and the mountain towering above us on the other, with the car getting slower and slower. There were times when we held our breath, as if in some way it lightened the load. My mind boggled at the thought that if the car couldn't make it, I would have to back all the way down to the bottom again — but it always did.

We passed through the lovely little Principality of Andorra in the Pyrenees and then started our slow zigzag descent down the other side through forests into Spain. Eventually we were down the other side and making our way across the hot Spanish countryside towards the Costa Brava and loving every minute of it. As we explored the coastline we came across a small signpost pointing along a narrow lane to Tossa de Mar. We had learned over the years that the best places are usually off the beaten track and we decided to have a look at the place. It turned out to be a beautiful, sleepy little fishing village, with the sea so clear and blue it almost mesmerized us. Since most of the roads in the place were more like narrow lanes running down between the houses towards the sea, and barely wide enough for vehicles, we soon discovered the best way to move about the place was to walk, otherwise bicycles appeared to be the best alternative within the connective network. We found a small hotel near the seafront but it was full and the Manager directed us to another house on the outskirts of the village where there was a vacancy for a couple of nights, which included breakfasts, so we booked in there. Our room was large, clean and sparsely furnished. The floors were tiled and the walls were painted white. A crucifix hung over the large double bed. In the corner of the room stood a huge, dark wooden wardrobe with roughly carved patterns on its doors. By its side stood a marble-topped table with a bowl and a jug of water.

That night we found a small restaurant near the seafront for our evening meal and sat at one of the

169

many tables outside. The air was warm with a slight breeze coming off the sea and later we strolled beneath a starlit sky along the water's edge, before slowly climbing back up through the narrow streets to our bed for the night.

The next day when Sally and I were sat on the beach eating our lunch of freshly cooked lobster, which we had bought from one of the local fishermen, we got into conversation with a fellow traveller who told us he had just vacated his room at the hotel where we had first tried to find accommodation on our arrival. He was having one last look at the sea before his departure, he said, and if we were quick we might be able to move into it. Straightaway we walked across to the hotel and found the room was still available and we booked in for the rest of the week. Then, feeling a bit uncomfortable about the situation, we went and collected our stuff from the other place. The owners didn't seem particularly surprised or upset at our move and we couldn't help thinking there was some kind of arrangement between the two places.

Our new room was no bigger than our earlier one, but the facilities were better and the dining room for its guests, although not very large, was quite impressive. It was overseen by the Maître d'Hôtel, a very stately middle-aged Spanish woman who, we noticed, never smiled the whole time we were there. Far from being rude or unpleasant, though, she was very correct and polite and took her job very seriously, ever watchful of everything that happened in the room whilst she was in charge. She stood in front of a large table which held additional condiments, napkins and menus, just inside the entrance. From there she could direct the staff easily. It was obvious she liked a smooth running operation with appropriate behaviour from everyone — both waiters and the guests!

The food was delicious and the only thing that upset me was a dish which I really liked. It was called paella, and was served the second night we were there. Unfortunately it didn't like me and I was violently sick afterwards and had to stay in bed the following day. Sally said it couldn't have been the paella since nobody else had problems, but to be on the safe side I gave it a miss for the rest of our time there.

Tossa turned out to be full of history, with part of it a mediaeval area inside huge ruined walls of a castle with several towers still standing, on a headland at the end of the bay. The warm colour of the aged stone, the blue of the sea and the patches of dark green pine trees growing everywhere combined to make a beautiful picture.

One day we went to Barcelona. We had heard that there was to be a bullfight that day and we thought we might go to see the spectacle. There was no mistaking the bullring when we saw it. "*Arenas de Barcelona*" was written over the main doorway. We were squeezed into tiered seats, with people's feet at our backs, in the blazing sun. Not anticipating that we would stay long we had gone for the cheaper seats. The more expensive ones were in the shade and we soon realised that it would have been worth paying the extra money, since the people sitting there appeared to be able to leave

171

their seats if they wanted. We, on the other hand, were unable to leave ours until the end of the whole programme of six fights had taken place.

The pomp and ceremony of the event was quite striking with the initial sound of horns before a lively Pasodoble filled the air and a couple of black clothed men on horseback, named *Commissars*, sitting proudly in their saddles, entered the arena on horseback. Soon they were followed by the *matadors* in their traditional clothing of black tights, pink socks and hats like Admiral Nelson's, named a montera. After that followed the *picadors*, dressed in white, sitting astride a horse. Their animals were encased from their neck to their ankles in a thick protective bamboo basket shield known as a *peto*. The horse was also blindfolded with a red kerchief, presumably so that it wouldn't see what was coming.

I hadn't realised until that moment that each fight is judged on its merits, because someone sitting near us pointed out the judges to us. They were sitting in the shaded, more expensive seats in the stadium. We could see that some of the wives of the dignitaries were wearing traditional Spanish costumes with mantillas and Sally was smitten with their clothes.

"Bet those dresses took some making. Imagine — all those ruffles," she said, getting completely sidetracked from the main event. I couldn't. With all the bright colours, music, the sun beating on our backs, and the roar of the crowds getting louder by the minute, the air was too full of excitement to worry about a bit of dressmaking.

At the beginning of the fight a man came out into the arena holding a sign with information about the bull in the next fight. When it was born, its weight, and which ranch it came from. After walking around with it for everyone to see, it was then displayed at the side of the arena for reference.

At the same time the *matador* approached the judges and asked their permission to fight the bull. This appeared to be part of the bullfighting tradition and I wondered if they were ever refused, and if so what kind of reasons would there be to give a bull a last minute reprieve? Or could it be that the judges might believe the bullfighter did not meet the physical requirements, by appearing too fat or heavy and not likely to sidestep the beast quickly enough when needed? These questions were never answered because the *matador* automatically received the necessary permission and almost immediately the bull was released into the arena through a gate some distance away. This prompted the *cuadrillas*, the men whose job it was to stimulate the bull if it had lost interest in the event, or on other occasions to distract it, if it was getting too serious with the matador too early in the piece, to start coming out from behind their barriers. These hiding places are spaced out regularly around the arena and, since the bull reacts to any movement, the bull was soon moving around the arena, from one barrier to another, displaying all his ferocity and strength to the eager crowd.

The bull was everything we had been told to expect. It was big, black and very mad, with a bulging huge muscle between its shoulders, looking something like a giant mad dog with its hackles up. This muscle is called the *morillo* and we learned that it is the job of the *picadors* to weaken this muscle enough so that the *matador* can put his sword through it into the bull's heart with one thrust and kill it.

In the beginning the *matador* placed his pink cape across a wooden stick, straightened up, and shouted "*Toro!*" The animal must have been trained with that word because it really enraged him and it tore across the arena at the matador, who neatly stepped to the side at the last minute. The closer he was to the bull the louder the cheers and the chorus of "*Olé*".

When the *matador* changed his pink cape for the red one, we knew the end was near and within a short time the bull lay dead on the floor and then a team of horses dragged its body out of the arena.

With another five fights before us we hoped it would all be over quickly. Two fulfilled our wishes and one showed us how angry the crowd could get if it thought the *matador* didn't come up to scratch. They booed and hissed him so loudly they probably heard it back in Tossa. I'm not sure what he did wrong. As far as I was concerned anybody who went into the arena with a mad animal needed to have their head looked at. He was obviously deemed by the regulars to be a coward of some kind, because to prove his courage he flamboyantly knelt on the floor with his cape and challenged the bull to charge him. At the last minute he still managed to lean his body out of the way. With this demonstration of valour the spectators went wild — he was forgiven.

Later I learned that when the spectators are particularly pleased with the bullfighter's performance they will indicate they wish one of the bull's ears to be cut off and presented to him. The president, mayor or chief dignitary sitting in the presidential box responds to their wishes by indicating his approval and the deed is done. If the performance was outstanding two ears might be given and on very, very exceptional circumstances part of the tail would also be given. Occasionally bulls will not fight. The problem then is to get the bull back out of the arena when some aren't keen on leaving. That's when a cow is brought in and the bull is encouraged to follow it out — and eventually does.

Prior to the bullfight the animals are kept on some sort of farm a short drive from the city. They are not fed from about 24 hours prior to the event and kept in almost total darkness in a steel enclosure with just a door at one end. The animals have always been nurtured and treated like kings up until this time, like a top racehorse, in preparation for their quarter of an hour of glory and, sadly, pain on the sand of the arena under the hot sun. The sudden deprivation of everything they were used to enrages them so much that they will throw themselves against the door in a frenzy to get out. When I heard about their treatment I could understand why the bulls that we saw were all fired up when they entered the arena.

The dressing procedure for bullfighters and pre-fight activities are very ritualised. Each man has his own dresser who assists him, since his costume is so tight he wouldn't manage alone and, after dressing, the bullfighter spends time in the chapel which every bullring has. There is also a fully equipped operating theatre in all major city bullrings.

I was told that even though it is still an uneven contest — man against beast — man does not always come out the total victor. It is still a dangerous occupation and most bullfighters experience a lot of fear in the arena.

At the end of the session we were really glad to leave and Sally and I agreed that we never wanted to see another bullfight. All we wanted at that moment was a cool drink and something to eat and not long afterwards we found ourselves in a restaurant, which had as entertainment a group of Spanish gypsy dancers. They appeared just like the ones I had seen in photographs, which I had recently come across in an old edition of a National Geographic Magazine. Sally had also seen the photographs and had anticipated with relish the thought of seeing the dancers in the flesh, so to speak.

The dancers were dressed in brightly coloured dresses with frills cascading everywhere and the men were dressed in full white shirts, with black trousers so tight that they looked like a second skin. Their black shoes had solid Cuban heels. Several men played guitars whilst they danced. There was lots of swirling of dresses and stamping of feet when the women danced, hands held high as they clicked their castanets, heads tilted backwards following the arch of their back, their faces showing great dedication.

The main male dancer was even more dramatic than the women when he danced. Starting with a slow, quiet click of his heels on the stone floor, he gradually increased the beat until he was slowly rotating the soles of his feet. And as his heels rapped the floor faster and faster he arched his back even more, drawing his eyebrows together intensely in response. Everyone's eyes were upon him. The louder it got, the more the expression of pain grew across his face. It was clear that he was pushing himself to the limit of his endurance and the guitar players cried out spontaneously in support, releasing some deep, hidden passion. The music grew stronger, louder, reverberating around the room. The air was electric.

Then Sally got sidetracked.

"He looks like he really means it, doesn't he?" she whispered, completely spoiling the whole thing.

As we left Tossa at the end of the week we determined to return the following year. It was the best holiday we had ever had — and cheap too — and although the hotel hadn't been large, it was comfortable, the food delicious, and worthy of many more visits. Little did we know, though, as we drove out along the narrow roads back onto the main road, that our holiday experience was far from over.

While we were still in Spain the roads were very quiet and we only saw one other car after we left Tossa. It was about mid-morning and we were heading back to

Andorra when we passed through a small village. A short distance from it was a hill and, when we started to descend it on the other side, we came across a man on his bicycle in front of us, wobbling all over the road. Each time he pulled over and I tried to pass him he would ride in front of the car again. This went on for a while and Sally and I couldn't understand what he was doing. Eventually he seemed to make a point of staying over on one side of the road and I slowly edged forward to pass him. Then he fell off his bicycle, sprawling across the road and ended up spreadeagled on his back on a dry dusty verge at the side of the road. I stopped the car and Sally and I went to help him. He couldn't speak any English and we couldn't speak any Spanish, but groaning is the same in any language and he was obviously in some pain. He appeared to be injured in some way and we had to do something to help him, but as far as we were concerned we hadn't touched him and we hoped he thought the same, otherwise, I thought, we might be in a predicament.

"Stay here with him, Sally," I said. "I'll drive back to the last village and get help, but don't move from this spot whatever happens."

I quickly found the local policeman, who fortunately could speak a little English, and I told him what had happened and offered to take him to the scene of the accident, and he agreed. When we returned to the scene of the accident the injured man was still laid out by the side of the road exactly as I had left them.

"He seems to be in a lot of pain," Sally said as we approached.

178

The policeman quickly sat by the man and questioned him for a couple of minutes before attempting to move him. At the end of it he appeared satisfied that we had nothing to do with it, which gave us a great sense of relief. The man began to move a bit now and although he was obviously hurting, it appeared that nothing was broken, and that bad bruising was the cause of his pain.

"His bicycle, senor," said the policeman. "It has no brakes. That is why he rides it like he did. Like the roads down a mountain — ziggy-zaggy." He waved his hand from side to side to demonstrate. It made sense now.

We were asked if we could take them both back to the village and we agreed and soon we were being directed to the man's home. As soon as we pulled up outside his house his wife came running out, becoming obviously upset when she saw her husband in such a state and viewed us with great suspicion. The policeman tried to calm her down and explain what happened but you could see that her husband wouldn't be working for a couple of days and from the look of the circumstances they would miss the money.

We felt very sorry for the couple and Sally and I had a quick conversation about what money we had to spare to help them, allowing for the rest of our journey home. In the end I put five pounds into his hand, but he was too proud, pushing it back into my hand, thanking us but shaking his head at the same time. His wife, however, fully realising their position, felt

179

differently about it and quickly took the money from me and put it into her pocket.

By the time we arrived home we had one pound left between us.

Later Sally said, "Just imagine if we'd got ourselves arrested, we'd 'ave never lived it down. I can just see the newspaper 'eadlines now: 'Local couple seized in Spain'."

The following year we returned to Tossa and I was tempted once more to try paella. Perhaps Sally was right, I thought, when she said it wasn't that which made me so ill. But again I had the same reaction and lost another day of my holiday lying in bed recovering. This time Sally believed me!

Over the next couple of years Tossa became our regular holiday spot and the journey enjoyable and uneventful except for the year we were pulled up by a police car in rural France. We had no idea what for and asked them. The two policemen, who were acting officiously, ignored our question and demanded to see our passports. Sally reached for them in her handbag and handed them over to the one who seemed to be in charge. Was this one of the scams I had been told about, I wondered? I had heard how some corrupt police would pull a car up for some fictitious reason and obtain a fine on the spot. If that happened I was told to say that you would pay the fine at the nearest police station, and ask them the directions to it. Chances were they would let you off at that point, as they did to a friend of ours, which confirmed your suspicions. This time, however, the leader of the two called his partner away from the car when he opened my passport. After a brief discussion they returned, smiling broadly.

"Ah," said the leader, reaching into the car and shaking my hand. "Please forgive us for stopping you. We did not realise you work for the Security Police." They spoke as if I was in charge of the British National Security — and I didn't bother to correct them. "Where are you going to?" he asked and I told him. "Follow us. We will escort you through to the other side of the next town." With that they took off in front of us and once on the other side they pulled over to let us pass, giving us big waves as we left.

But each year there were more people at Tossa. Then one year we went and there was an English fish and chip shop opened on the beach front not far from our hotel. We never returned to Tossa after that. My favourite meal is fish and chips and we lived opposite a fish and chip shop at home, but when we went to Spain we wanted Spanish food — providing it wasn't paella. For us, Tossa de Mar had lost its uniqueness and had been spoiled.

CHAPTER
TWENTY-TWO

When Topper Went
Over the Top

The Monday after we returned from holidays I went to the local cattle market to have a look for some weaners — baby pigs — that I could fatten up and sell again later. I'd sold my last lot before we went on holidays, which helped pay for our trip, and I was keen to restock. Sometimes, in the past, I had bought a pregnant sow and waited to see what nature delivered. Other times I kept a sow from a litter I had fattened up for market and sent her off to a stud. This turned out to be a task and a half by the time I put a ring through her nose so that I could guide her with a rope along the alley, under the railway tunnel, past the foundry and eventually into a waiting truck. The sow was always delighted with its sense of freedom as we walked along and was keen to investigate her surroundings, much to the consternation and some amusement of any cyclists using the alley.

I often wondered if the pigs remembered making the same journey along the alley when they were brought home from the markets, like a dog can remember its way around. The pigs did enough sniffing and snuffling around to match them any day. Of course it would have depended how big they were when I bought them, because if they were really young it was too far for them to walk and I always carried them. It was only when they were bigger that they would be herded along in a bunch. When that happened it usually ended with at least one of them making a run for it into the foundry, but they never got very far. There were too many willing foundry hands looking for a bit of fun and I never lost one.

The first time I had a sow in farrow was very exciting, and I spent much time setting up her sty for a safe delivery, like making sure that she had a clean bed of straw. Although contrary to the popular myth, I always found that pigs were very clean animals. They never fouled their sleeping area and always kept their beds clean. Also I put a farrowing rail in place, where the piglets could escape their mother's bulk if she suddenly turned over. There were about eight in the first litter. And the day after they arrived — they were born in the middle of the night — Jill and Sally came and stood at the foot of the sty, admiring the new additions with so many "ooohs" and "ahhhs" you would have thought they were visiting the local maternity hospital.

This time on my visit to the markets, however, I decided to buy pigs which had already been weaned and headed for that section. The market was packed with people and animals that morning. It was extra muddy underfoot, having rained earlier that morning, and was definitely wellington boots territory. The auctioneer was already doing a brisk trade nearby, his voice necessarily loud to make himself heard above the general cacophony. I spent some time walking between the pens, checking them over before the bidding started. There were lots of small pigs for sale that morning, and all of them keen on letting us know they were there, with squeals and screams that only hungry little piglets can make.

"See anything yer like, Bill?" I turned and saw Topper Jones.

Topper was a large man and probably in his early forties at that time. He was the eldest son of Mrs. Jones, the publican of the County Arms in Millbrook Street, and always appeared to be a quiet man. Someone you might refer to as a gentle giant.

Since his father had died Topper had helped his mother with the pub and did all the heavy work around the place. His mother, Mrs. Jones, was still very agile for her age, as she must have been near retirement age at the time and still rode her upright bicycle everywhere to do her shopping. For years she had been a regular customer at the dry-cleaning shop where Sally worked, often arriving with an overloaded bicycle of her family's clothes to be cleaned. Sally liked her a lot, not because of the business she brought to the shop, but because Mrs. Jones would always stop and have an entertaining story to tell about her family or the pub.

"There's a couple of lots I'm interested in. What about you?" I asked

"I'm after some eggs for the pub," he said.

"'ow's it going?" I asked. The County always had a good regular crowd.

"'ad a bit of trouble last night but soon sorted it out."

I waited to hear what kind of trouble it was, but the auctioneer was suddenly standing over the lot I was interested in and Topper gave a quick cheerio and headed for the poultry section. I thought no more about our brief conversation until later that day when I bumped into a good mate of mine, Roy Folkes. He was about the same age as me and lived in Alfred Street.

" Did yer 'ear about last night in the pub?" he asked. I knew he was a regular drinker at the County.

"Topper said there was a bit of trouble." I said.

"Bet 'e never told yer what 'e did, though. Knowing Topper, 'e'd never brag but 'e was bloody marvellous."

"What d'yer mean?"

"Let's say 'e sorted some blokes out,"

"I always thought of 'im as a gentle giant who wouldn't 'arm a fly," I remarked.

"So did I until last night!" laughed Roy, his eyes almost watering with the thought of it.

"Well, what 'appened?" I said, getting more curious by the minute.

"There were three of 'em — blokes we'd never seen before, definitely not regulars. They were 'aving a glass of cider and playing the jukebox. At first nobody took any notice of them, but the trouble was they started getting on everybody's nerves because they kept playing the same song over and over and over. Then to make matters worse they started singing as well, which

185

wouldn't have been so bad if they could sing but they couldn't — and that got louder and louder. You can imagine all the regulars were getting a bit fed up with it. Yer could 'ardly 'ear yerself talk. Anyway, the old lady could see which way the wind was blowing and turned down the sound a bit on the jukebox. That's when things turned nasty, 'cos they started swearing at 'er to turn the bloody thing back on, and 'ow they'd be over the counter to turn it on themselves if she didn't do it, and what they'd do to 'er if she forced 'em to do that. You can imagine 'ow we all felt. It was starting to get really nasty. They were old enough to be our sons and looked twice as strong. Reckon they were navvies or something like that. All I know is neither me nor m'mates would've stood a chance with 'em and I was trying to think what to do.

"Course, they thought the old lady was on 'er own be'ind the bar — and so did we. But unknown to us Topper was bent down behind the counter putting some bottles away. Well, when 'e 'eard their language aimed at 'is mother, 'e went berserk. No word of a lie, Bill, 'e cleared the counter in one leap — I've never seen anything like it. All of us regulars moved to the sides of the room, just like in one of them western films, when there's going to be a gunfight. Course, it was the last thing the three blokes expected and when they saw 'im they all turned, and in their panic all 'eaded for the door at the same time and all three got jammed together in the doorway. Then two of 'em managed to push through, but Topper caught the third and gave 'im an 'elping 'and. It was bloody marvellous to watch." Roy's eyes shone with the memory of it.

"Topper's normally such a quiet bloke, too," I said.

"That's right, but them blokes really set 'im off, last night, I can tell you. Talking to 'is mother like they did — 'e wouldn't take that from anybody."

"So a good time was 'ad by one and all," I laughed. "You don't usually get live entertainment like that round Millbrook Street!"

"That's right, and when Topper came back in we all gave him three cheers and the old lady gave us all drinks on the 'ouse — to get over it!"

187

CHAPTER
TWENTY-THREE

An Incident at the Butcher's Shop

One of the businesses working out of the Gloucester Depot was a mobile shop. In fact there were several of them. Whatever the weather they would travel far and wide to isolated villages in the Cotswolds and other surrounding areas, selling a wide range of foods. I was quite friendly with one of the drivers, a man named Jack Evans, who came from Newent. He was in his mid-forties, slim, and stood just under six feet tall, with a congeniality about him that well suited his job. Jack would often stop by for a chat or to share a funny story concerning his day's work, before heading home.

"I've just been to see if I can get my son a job in a butcher's shop in Gloucester," he told me one day. "He's working as a butcher's apprentice in the Newent branch at the moment, but he fancies having a change of scenery. You know how kids are when they want to spread their wings."

I agreed, remembering how Gloucester had felt too small for me when I was young. Newent was a lot smaller.

"That would be good if he gets it; then he could travel in with you each day," I said.

"That's what I thought," said Jack.

"Well, how did it go — did you have any luck?"

"Yes, they've offered him a job as an apprentice butcher at Barton Street. He'll be over the moon." From the smile on Jack's face he was already over it.

In due course his son started his new position with Jack proudly briefing us, over the following weeks, on his progress. All seemed well for a while until one day, when he stopped for a chat, he wasn't his usual upbeat self.

"That's buggered," he said, looking worried. " I don't think my son's going to last in that job."

"Why?" I asked.

"Oh, the job's all right and there's nothing wrong with his work, but yesterday a couple of Irish blokes, who use the Vauxhall Pub, went into the shop and asked for some steak. They wanted five pounds worth, they said. The kid cut the meat and weighed it and then wrapped it up, but instead of handing over the money, one of the blokes reached over and threatened him before grabbing the meat and running out of the shop. Laughing their heads off, apparently."

"That's no good — what about the butcher in charge, what did he do?" I said, already wondering why it hadn't been sorted out.

"Nothing. What could he do? Besides, I think he was in the freezer at the time, so the kid was on his own on the front counter and there were no other customers in the shop."

"They wouldn't try a stunt like that if there were other people around." I wished I'd been there.

"That's right — and when I picked him up last night he was really scared," Jack said. "The whole thing has frightened him to death. I don't know what to do about it."

This wouldn't have happened if the previous butcher had still been there, I thought. His name was Harry Taylor, a powerfully built man with a personality to match. He could look after himself and any shop, anywhere. In other words, he could be formidable when required. Harry was now working at the Robinswood branch and I told Fred about him.

"He was in charge of that shop before" I said, "and there was never any trouble then. Why don't you get in touch with him and tell him about this incident? Who knows, I wouldn't be surprised if he felt like having a bit of fun, he would agree to go back to Barton Street for a while. It would be right up his alley. If he wants to do it, he could easily sort it out with his boss."

We learned later that when Harry Taylor was told about the two Irishmen, it resurrected some memories and he was keen to return to Barton Street to help sort out the two thieves. Whether he felt like having a bit of fun, or that Robinswood was too quiet for him — or both — I don't know, but his transfer was soon arranged. Meanwhile, Jack's son was sent back to Newent.

It was about a fortnight later when the depot was suddenly abuzz with news of an incident which had just taken place in the butcher's shop in Barton Street that

190

afternoon. The story of what happened was told and retold over the following weeks with all the relish, fervour and generosity it deserved, and over the ensuing years entered the company's folklore.

It appeared that the two steak thieves, after having taken their fill at the Vauxhall, across the road, thought they might try their luck again for a free supper and had returned to the scene of their former crime, completely unaware that their little game was about to come to an abrupt end. Harry, being the astute man that he was, had already prepared himself for the event — which he knew was sure to take place sooner or later — by placing one of his choppers on a shelf below the counter where it was within easy reach.

As before, the two men waited outside the shop until it was empty before entering, and the moment Harry set eyes on them his natural born instincts told him they were the ones and when they spoke his suspicions were confirmed.

"Five quidsh of frying shteak!" slurred one of the men, giving a sideways grin to his mate, who gave a knowing smirk back.

Harry took his time cutting the meat, which made the thief edgy and caused him to sneer: "Talk about bloody 'quick service'!"

"Yair," said the other keeping his eye on the shop door.

Slowly Harry weighed the meat and wrapped it.

"That'll cost you a fiver," said Harry.

At this point one of the blokes reached across the counter to grab the parcel, the same as he did before —

but Harry was too quick for him. With the speed, cunning, and tenacity of a champion of the martial arts, Harry pinned the thief's wrist to the counter with one hand while he grabbed his chopper from under the counter with the other. Holding his highly sharpened weapon in the air ready to strike, no doubt with the speed of lightning if required, Harry yelled:

"EITHER YOU PAY ME A FIVER OR I'LL HAVE YOUR F . . . G HAND OFF!"

On hearing these menacing words and perhaps wondering if he was having a touch of the "DTs", the second bloke made a run for it, leaving his mate still pinned to the counter in Harry's vice-like grip.

"YOU 'EARD WHAT I SAID!" yelled Harry, reiterating his intentions.

His captive, fearing he was about to become a victim of a blood bath, became frantic to escape this barbaric end and desperately fumbled through his pockets with his free hand until he found some money, which he threw at Harry who immediately released him. Then the thief ran from the shop, leaving his meat on the counter.

After that there was no trouble in the shop again — but I can't remember if the boy from Newent ever came back.

CHAPTER
TWENTY-FOUR

Jill Gets Married

In 1958 Jill got married. She had met a Polish boy named Tadeusz Andruszkiewicz (Ted) several years earlier at a meeting of the International Friendship League held at a hall in Park Road, close to where Ted was lodging at the time. Jill and her friend Vicki Pesce went to the meetings regularly, even going to Switzerland on a holiday with the group. He seemed a nice bloke to Sally and me, but reservations started to kick in when we realized that they were getting serious about each other.

"Are you sure you know what you're doing?" Sally asked Jill one day. "There's nothing wrong with Ted but he's not like us. He's from another part of the world — they do things differently, they've got different ways."

"What things? Do you mean he eats food with his feet?" laughed Jill, dismissing our concerns.

The truth was we didn't know his family background, where he was brought up, who his associates were, and it worried us. With only one child we were over-protective. As it turned out there were no grounds for our fears. We couldn't have had a better son-in-law.

Not long after they married they bought a house in Vauxhall Road and when our two grandchildren arrived everything seemed perfect, so the news that they were again considering emigrating to Australia came as a surprise, and disappointment. I say "again" because they had first talked about it when they got engaged, thinking they might emigrate and marry in Australia. But because Ted wasn't a British subject at that time they would have had to emigrate separately and the idea was shelved — permanently, we had hoped.

It wasn't long before they were having their interviews and medicals, and on a cold winter's day Sally and I, accompanied by Ted's younger brother, Roman, waved them goodbye at Southampton.

CHAPTER
TWENTY-FIVE

Australia

Jill wrote us letters all the way through their journey, keeping us up to date on everything — the sea voyage, their arrival in Melbourne and experiences in a migrant hostel, also Ted's various jobs as he searched for the right position. They were told they could stay at the hostel for up to two years if they needed to, to help them settle in their new country. He had a job to go to, but the migrant hostel they were sent to was too far away from it and he soon found another one closer.

Sally and I eagerly read their stories of adventures in their new country. We heard how they bought their first car — Ted had already taken driving lessons in England before they left — their trips into the Great Dividing Range in winter when it snowed, and the heat of a Melbourne summer.

About eighteen months after they arrived, Jill wrote and told us that Ted had got a new job with a mining company named Hamersley Iron, which was opening up a new town, Dampier, on the remote northwest coast of Australia. He would be working as a rolling stock fitter and he was told that there would be a brand new house provided for them. They were both very excited at the prospect. It was something they had been looking for. Jill said that living in a Melbourne suburb hadn't really appealed to them on a long-term basis. They preferred it in the countryside, but finding work there was the problem. Providing he liked it, this new job sounded perfect and with a new house by the sea to go with it, what else could they ask for?

Regular letters told us that Ted had flown ahead to take up his new position whilst his house was being completed and it was five months later when Jill and the two children joined him. On the way they stopped off for a week in Perth, the capital of Western Australia, where they stayed with her friend Vicki and her family who had also emigrated there, before catching the plane north.

Soon we were hearing about their new place and how much they liked it. It was hot they said, but the houses were all air-conditioned and after they had settled in Jill asked when we were going out to visit them. We decided that Sally would go; she could manage to get a couple of months off from work, whereas I would have found it difficult. Besides, there were the pigs to look after. They weren't due for market yet and there was no one I could ask at that time to help out.

Vicki met Sally when she arrived in Perth and looked after her for a couple of days before putting her on a plane for the North West. From the moment Sally touched down she was enchanted with the country, and when she arrived in Dampier her letters overflowed with news and enthusiasm for the place. It was a wonderful adventurous way of life, she said.

Meanwhile I decided to take advantage of her absence and decorate the house from top to bottom. It needed freshening up and I thought it would be a nice homecoming for her when she returned. I studied the wallpaper books and the paint charts over the following week, calculating the amount I required, then went and bought the whole lot. From then on I spent all my free time redecorating, starting at the top of the house and working my way down. At the end of five weeks I had finished it and at the end of the sixth the smell of turps had cleared the air. A week later I drove up to Heathrow Airport to meet Sally.

When she entered the Arrival Lounge there was no doubt she had spent some time in the sunshine. She was wearing a beautiful golden tan; she always went brown in the sun, different to Jill and me — we always went pink. Our journey back home seemed to fly as she filled me in with the latest news, how much the grandchildren had grown, how happy Jill and Ted were, and how she had loved every minute of it.

In all the letters I had written to her while she was away, I never once mentioned about my redecorating the house — I wanted it to be a nice surprise. So when we got home and she walked into the house I waited to hear her comments but she said nothing. After about half an hour, when we'd had time to make ourselves comfortable and were sipping a cup of hot tea, I could wait no longer.

"Is there anything different about the house, since you went away?" I asked.

"Yes," she said. "Whatever made you choose battleship grey paint?"

It took another six weeks to rectify.

My first visit to Australia happened after I finished work. It had been suggested by everyone that we should plan our visit so that we could all be together at Christmas time. Sally had already finished work and my retirement couldn't come quick enough in her eagerness to return. A friend offered to drive us to Heathrow and when we arrived Sally gave him her fur coat to take back to Gloucester.

The long haul flight was very enjoyable and we only stopped for refuelling. As we approached Perth I was surprised to see how much clear land there was still below us. Different to London where everything is more densely populated and spread out.

Jill had arranged overnight accommodation for us at a hotel named Miss Maud's in Perth, before we took the next part of our journey north, approximately 1600 kms. My first impression of the city was how light, bright and clean it was with streets much wider than the ones I was used to, and how friendly everybody was. It was also very warm and I wondered how much hotter it was going to be when we arrived at our final destination. I didn't like the heat, but consoled myself with the thought that nothing could be worse than the sirocco, the hot, oppressive and often dusty wind that I experienced in North Africa during the war. If I could survive that I could survive anything.

Our flight north departed about midday and was scheduled to be just over two hours in duration. As we flew further and further north into the tropics, the view through my aircraft window told me everything I needed to know, with the earth below slowly changing from green to gold, and then to golden oranges, pinks and mauves. Occasional riverbeds coursed through it like dark veins and distant rugged ranges of blue hills folded down on to the coastal plain.

When we eventually started to descend, I looked again out of the window, hoping to see some sign of civilization, but there was none. In the haze to the left there was the distant sea and to the right more distant hills. Then, as we flew lower, I could see a dirt track and railway line ahead. The next thing we were flying over the track and could see another road on the other side, a sealed one this time. Suddenly we were landing with a bump on a runway in the middle of nowhere. A small building and a tower flashed past on my left as we touched down, but otherwise there was no sign of human habitation in any direction.

"Is this it?" I asked Sally, not believing it could be. With any luck it was just a refuelling stop.

"Yes — we're here!" said Sally, with excitement. "You're going to love it." I wasn't so sure.

I was trying to be enthusiastic about it as I looked through the aircraft's window, but all I could see was red dust with tufts of grass the colour of straw, red rocks, and a hot sun beating down. Was this Earth or Mars? The place looked vast and empty, just like I'd seen in a recent western movie; in fact I wouldn't have

199

been surprised to see John Wayne racing towards me on his horse, or Apache Indians cresting the distant flat top hills.

The plane reached the end of the runway, turned around and started to taxi slowly back towards the small building and there outside, waving frantically, were Jill and the children. A few minutes later we were climbing down the steps and hugging each other.

"This wasn't here last time," said Sally, pointing to the building and sounding like a seasoned traveller to the area.

"It's our new airport! Beats having a lonely sentry box standing all on its own, in the middle of nowhere, doesn't it?" laughed Jill.

"Sentry box?" I asked.

"Well, it looked like it but it was a toilet," said Sally.

"Or dunny as they called it here," laughed Jill.

The journey into Dampier took us across a causeway to the island on which the town was built. On both sides of the road were saltpans containing white crystallizing seawater so bright it stung my eyes. It seemed hotter, too, as we drove along and the distant horizon to our right quivered. Jill was working for Dampier Salt, the owner of the salt works, at that time.

I looked ahead at the island. It looked like it was made of only rocks, big red ones mostly, all piled high on top of each other, as if thousands of years ago there had been an eruption and all the rocks had been disgorged from somewhere deep down in the earth. Patches of spinifex could be seen clinging to the steep sides of the hills, where enough dust had blown to give the spiky grass a foothold. Miraculously, small trees could be seen sprouting from between rocks where a few drops of rainwater had given them a chance of life. On the other side of the causeway we climbed a steep hill and when we reached the top passed through a cutting with tall rock walls on both sides. A moment later the sea came into full view.

"There you are," said Sally. "Just like I told you. Isn't it beautiful?"

And what was the good of a blue sea if you couldn't swim in it because of sharks, I thought — already feeling miserable without one piece of moist green foliage in sight.

Jill gave us a quick tour of the town by taking the road along the foreshore. In the distance we could see the jetty with a huge ship being loaded with iron ore. Then we passed the large camp of transportable buildings, which was accommodation for the single men working for the company. After that was a small general store adjoining a large metal shed with several large doors in the side of it. And in the front was a gravel forecourt with numerous tables and benches.

"Is that a workshop?" I asked, pointing at the shed.

"No," laughed Jill. "That's the Wet Mess. The place where the blokes go for a drink after work."

I took a second look.

"What — in there?" I said.

"Yes — they open those big doors and there's a long bar inside. The blokes can go there straight from work, if they want, in their working clothes. A lot of the men work such long hours that when they finish work all they want is a cold beer, a meal, a shower and a good bed to sleep in. If they had to spruce themselves up each night and walk into the townsite for a drink I reckon there would be an uprising. The company would probably lose half of their workers overnight! If you and Mum feel like going out for a drink one night you don't have to worry, there's always the Mermaid Hotel in town — it's new and you'd like it."

Opposite the Wet Mess was the water desalination plant and then still more transportable units as we drove further along the bay. Then for a short distance there were no buildings on either side until on the right, between the road and the sea, I could see a fenced compound with rows and rows of seats set out in front of what looked like a large white billboard.

"That's our cinema," Jill said.

Suddenly houses came into sight on the left, whilst we continued our journey along the seafront until we came to a fenced-off swimming area in the sea.

"Don't worry — it's shark proof," Jill said.

Next we were climbing a hill past houses and a small cluster of shops. The houses in the town were built on the side of a hill, all facing the sea.

"How did they manage to build these houses with all these rocks?" I asked, thinking about the time years ago, when I had dug ditches for a living, and how difficult the job would be here.

"All the soil that was needed had to be brought into town by truck," said Jill. "When we first got here the trucks were running continuously with loads of it. It was needed for the house pads, the roads and everything else. Even now, although there are lawns growing everywhere which helps to stabilize the soil and stops it from being blow away, it's only shallow. If you try to dig in the garden you'll find it's rock about a foot down. But the company is very good and will send anybody a truckload of topsoil if a person orders it. Of course it's up to you to spread it on your garden. Some people have made 'contained veggie patches'."

" 'Contained veggie patches'?" I asked.

"Yes. They sometimes put four or eight railway sleepers in a square and fill in the centre with soil. It's enough for a small patch. Others settle for old truck tyres from the massive vehicles they use at the mine and fill those and grow things."

The surrounding countryside looked so dry I found it difficult to imagine anything growing in that environment, although I had to admit that several of the gardens looked quite green and lush.

A short time later we were entering their driveway and saw the accommodation that Hamersley Iron Pty. Ltd. provided for their employees. By English standards it was a very large bungalow and the inside of it was surprisingly good, with three bedrooms, a kitchen, a bathroom — and a laundry. It was also fully furnished. For the first time since our arrival I was impressed.

I soon learned that Dampier was named after William Cecil Dampier, who was the first Englishman to visit Australia. He was also a buccaneer, though it appears that he joined the pirates out of curiosity more than his desire for wealth, and ended up writing about his adventures. His was the first recorded visit by any

203

European to the region, in 1699, which was a surprise since I had always thought it was Captain Cook was the first. The difference is, I suppose, that Captain Cook was the one who planted a flag and claimed the country for Britain. Dampier's name was also given to the Dampier Archipelago, a series of about 42 islands and rocks lying to the west and north of the town.

The coastal town of Dampier was built in the 1960s as a port for the iron ore mines at Tom Price and Paraburdoo over 290 kms inland. The ore is railed to the port where it is stockpiled, blended and loaded onto ore carriers that ship it to ports around the world. Massive things they were, too, as they glided into the port, sitting high in the water when entering, lying low with their load when they left.

Over the following weeks Jill and Ted took us to the local places of interest such as Roebourne about 45 kms away, which is the oldest town between Port Gregory, another historic town approximately 1200 kms south, and Darwin in the Northern Territory. It was established in 1864 and named after John Septimus Roe.

Another place close by was a ghost town named Cossack. The town was first settled in 1863 and was home to a thriving pearling industry as well as a multicultural population of adventurers and treasure hunters. By the turn of the century, however, the pearling fleet had moved to Broome. Cossack used to be the main port for the North West before it became silted up. After that the shipping facilities moved to

Point Samson, a short distance away — a delightful little place with a safe lagoon in the bay for swimming.

Cossack had a very grand, well-preserved courthouse and bond store. It was the same with the Shire Offices and Prison in Roebourne. Someone said that it was always a priority to show that Law and Order prevailed when settling a new port or town and the building of impressive courthouses and prisons was one way of reinforcing that. The law had to be shown to prevail at all costs because new towns attracted all kinds of people, good and bad, and without strict law enforcement a new town would not survive in a pioneering country like this.

Caution had to be taken when visiting Cossack, however, because of the tides. If you weren't careful and didn't check the tidal charts before you left, you could find yourself cut off for about six hours until the water receded.

"It only happened to us once," said Jill. "That was when we first got up here and weren't familiar with these sorts of things. Now the tides are a way of life with us."

Just the short time I had been there I realised how true that was. For a start the tide chart was always on the front of the fridge with special notations on the low tides, because that was the time the family went shelling.

The case for law and order and the keeping of it also applied to Dampier. But the company had a quick solution for any troublemakers. The culprits were given 24 hours to leave town and if they happened to be held in the lock-up overnight after initiating or even participating in a brawl at the wet mess or the Mermaid the previous evening, they were dropped off on the outskirts of town — on the other side of the causeway — by the police the following morning. From there they had to find their own way to wherever they wanted to go. What with the heat and everything, I thought it all sounded a bit harsh and drastic when I heard about it. But, as Ted said, nobody was heard of dying from heat exhaustion and the culprit would most likely have got a lift with a long distance lorry if he could make it to the north-west coastal highway about 20 kms away. Even then he would have to be lucky because the traffic moved in a wave and if you didn't catch it you might have to wait hours before another vehicle passed by. Port Hedland was about a three hours' drive north of the Dampier turnoff, so providing you wanted to go south and were waiting at that spot about three hours after dawn, you had a good chance of getting a lift, because most of the trucks would have left at first light. It was the same if you wanted to go north. Carnarvon was about five hours south of the turnoff, so your best bet of getting a lift north would have been about five hours after sunrise.

At least by the time I got to visit, the main road was sealed. When Sally had visited the first time, the road was only sealed from Perth to just north of Carnarvon, which meant that when a cyclone passed by and dumped tonnes of water the roads became impassable, with road trains stuck for up to a week or more.

"Afterwards the roads looked like ploughed fields until the grader went through," said Ted.

Any road leading off the main road remained unsealed, and even when it hadn't rained there were rules to be quickly learned if you wanted to survive in such hostile territory. The first was to always carry sufficient fuel, plus 2 spare tyres, a repair kit, and *always* a large container of water (and a packet of biscuits) stored somewhere in the car. Also to let people know where you intended to go.

"So when does it actually rain?" I asked. We hadn't seen a spot of it since our arrival and I began to wonder if I would ever see it again.

"About two weeks at the beginning of August," said Jill. "That's the winter rains."

"Is that all?" I asked, my disappointment showing.

"The only other time is when a cyclone passes down the coast. There's usually about three or four each summer, after Christmas, but they're not always full of water. Sometimes they're more wind than wet."

While we were still in Dampier we experienced three cyclone warnings. The townsite was warned that a storm was heading our way and everybody set about battening down everything around their houses. The instruction given to residents, if they were caught outside when a cyclone hit, was to "crawl to higher ground and hang on".

"That's enough to frighten anybody to death even if the storm doesn't kill you," remarked Sally when she read it. Luckily we never experienced that level of storm. Each of the cyclones missed us and crossed on to land further down the coast, missing any inhabited areas and dumping much needed rain on the outback stations.

There had been a new town built since Sally's last visit — Karratha. Only about half an hour's drive away, it offered several new exciting shopping opportunities to the locals, although Jill and her friends reckoned it spoilt their trips to Perth.

"It used to be really exciting going to Perth after a period of twelve months or more, and going into the big shops again and having a good spending spree with the money we had saved for the trip. We'd come home loaded up with practically new wardrobes for everybody. Now, with Karratha and its large K-mart store, we just pop out to buy an item when we need it. It's handy and that's about all but the fun's gone out of shopping now."

Jill said even then there were some housewives who couldn't stand the isolation after living in a big city and occasionally it was the cause of family break-ups, where the husband wanted to stay but the wife became bored with nothing to do. This was the time before television was broadcast to the region and it depended on the housewives finding something to keep themselves busy. As for Jill, it turned out to be a blessing in disguise. It gave her the time to develop her love of art and acting, which she had always wanted to do.

Before Christmas we were given a big treat — we went to a pantomime. Ever since we had arrived, Jill and the children had been rehearsing the production. Jill was a founder member of the Dampier Repertory

Company and had been greatly involved with it ever since it was first formed shortly after they arrived in the town. We saw Ted spending a lot of his spare time building puzzling props for it — such as matching tables which could be pulled apart and put together again on stage and many other mysterious items, which appeared straight out of a fairytale book. There was much talk about the show's preparation at home, since Jill was producing and directing it, besides spending hours painting the scenery, but it was obvious they didn't want us to know too much about it beforehand. Sally and I commented to each other on the amount of work everybody seemed to be putting into it and began to wonder what to expect. In the end, considering the population of the town, we concluded it might be comparable to the endeavours of a small Cotswold village club, holding their Christmas panto in their local church hall, and we looked forward to the opening night with loyal anticipation.

The pantomime was being performed in the local Community Centre, a large imposing building in the centre of town and as we walked up the steps to enter we could see that it was already half full. To add to our astonishment there was a full live band already tuning up in front of the stage. In no time all the seats were taken and after that people started standing along the walls, some with their own collapsible chairs, while children with cushions were ushered to a space near the front where they could see. Sally and I looked at each other in amazement. We might have expected a full house at the Bristol Hippodrome — but Dampier?

The air was electric as the band started to tune up and the children were laughing excitedly. Then, under a big spotlight, the band let fly with a rollicking introduction and the big red velvet curtains were pulled aside and *Cinderella* began. And it was the best and funniest pantomime I had ever seen in my life — and I had seen quite a few over the years! Everybody was rolling in the aisles at the ugly sisters by the end of it. They were the best I had ever seen. Especially since I recognised one of them as a local fireman and father of the bandleader, and the other one a Safety Officer. There was also the added attraction of seeing our grandchildren performing with the puppets our grandson had made. The scenery was so well done. Jill said she looked upon painting it as a kind of apprenticeship. There was no-one else in town who would have attempted to paint it, so it was left entirely to her.

"I can design and paint it without any interference. Everybody in the Repertory is grateful for whatever I do and there's always somebody willing to fill in large blocks of colour when needed. Thankfully it always turned out all right. How lucky can a person be to have such an opportunity?"

And who would have thought she had to travel to the other side of the earth to fulfil her dream, I thought.

It turned out that the show was sold out for the whole week, packed every night. People came from far and wide. One family, off a local station named Cooya Pooya, about 80 kms away, never missed any of the local productions, especially pantomimes. They were

210

quite isolated and the children on the station were educated at home, so the Christmas Show was a special treat for them. Some children in town boasted that they saw the show every night.

We learned also that when the Repertory put on their annual Music Hall in the winter months, the local people would start queuing after work the night before the box office opened for the following morning at 9a.m. They camped overnight, to make sure they got their tickets and queuing became an annual event as well as the show. It was the time of the year when there were lots of visits from residents' families and many planned their visits to coincide with the production. The tickets were sold in tables of 10 seats and some groups would get together and do a roster amongst themselves to cover the hours of queuing. Others didn't mind — they took along their seats, blankets, radios, torches, books, food, drink and anything else, which would help to pass the time, and enjoyed the experience.

We had a lovely Christmas Day. It turned out that Jill, Ted and the children were good friends with another family from London, Laura and Joe Lopez and their children, who lived nearby, and had always spent their Christmases together at each other's houses in turn, ever since they had arrived in town. That year it was at Laura and Joe's and we had a wonderful time. Joe showed me his garden and proved what a variety of fruit and vegetables could be grown in the area. He even had a large grapevine growing over their back patio.

After Christmas the heat was even more intense and a couple of cyclone warnings were issued but we were lucky, they struck an area further down the coast. We did most of our sightseeing within the first couple of weeks of arrival because slowly the heat became overpowering and Sally and I resorted to staying in the air-conditioned house during the day, reading our books and only walking along the Dampier back beach in the evening when the cool breeze off the water was most welcome. The brilliantly coloured sunsets, as the sun dropped below the nearest island every evening, were beyond description.

It was just before Easter when we departed and, although it had been wonderful being with our family again, I had often cursed the heat and longed for the cool, moist, green pastures of home.

On the second day back in Gloucester it snowed.

CHAPTER
TWENTY-SIX

We Have to Move

When Sally and I were told we would have to move out
of our house to make way for a new motorway we were
devastated. We were in our seventies by then and had
lived at 130 Millbrook Street for most of our married
life and Sally had grown up there. Although it didn't
actually belong to us, it felt like it did. We had looked
after the place well over the years, regularly painting
and decorating it, and had made it into our own little
palace.

Earlier on in our married life our plan had been to
save enough money and buy a small cottage in the
country somewhere, but every time we thought we had
enough money we found that the prices of the cottages
had risen accordingly. It was a never-ending cycle. In
fact the thought of the dream cottage had slowly
slipped away and we had long since come to the
conclusion that 130 Millbrook Street was to be our
home forever, and as time went by we didn't mind one
bit. With my allotments to keep me busy and Sally
enjoying her retirement, you might say we were both
truly settled.

213

So when we were visited by a woman from the Council one day, who informed us that we were to be moved to a flat somewhere, Sally and I were not very pleased. In fact, to put it bluntly, we dug our heels in.

"We're not moving unless we like the place we're going to!" I told the woman.

"You don't have much choice," she said, totally irritated by such opposition. "These houses have got to go and you've got to move."

"I expect they 'ave," I said. "But we're not going somewhere we don't like. We'll stay 'ere until the bulldozers move in if we 'ave to!"

It was a stand-off and the woman left us in a bit of a huff.

The thought of living in a flat with no garden and possibly no allotments anywhere near had filled me with dread from the first mention of that type of dwelling. We were determined we didn't want to be put in a flat somewhere, surrounded by nothing but brick walls, cement, and lifts which constantly broke down.

About a week later we had another visitor and this time it was someone with more understanding and a kinder touch. It was a step in the right direction, and when we were asked what kind of place we would like, the anxiety that Sally and I had felt over the previous week started to ease a little.

"We would like something with a bit of ground on it," Sally said. "Bill would go mad without 'is bit of gardening — and I'd join 'im in no time."

"Leave it to me," the young woman said. "I can't promise anything but I'll see what I can find."

214

She was back a couple of days later with the choice of two places, both with a garden attached. We had a look at both and chose 8 Copperfield Close, Matson. It was a one-bedroom unit in a small pensioners' complex, with a small garden in the front and quite a large piece of ground at the back. I liked it the moment I saw it but Sally was a bit hesitant, frightened she would make the wrong decision. It was a lot bigger than we had expected and the living room was twice as big as our one at Millbrook Street with windows at both ends making it light and airy. An added novelty was that the kitchen was big enough to sit and eat your meals. Something we had never had before. The best bit of all, though, was a bathroom. Years earlier we had had a shower unit put into the second bedroom at 130. It looked something like a green telephone booth and the grandchildren referred to it as the Tardis, but it served the purpose and stopped us having to drag the old tin bath into the kitchen, and putting on the hot water boiler.

So the sight of the bathroom clinched the deal and when we had the quality carpet cleaned, which had been fitted by the previous tenant, we were eager to move. Thanks to Wally and his family the transfer was almost painless, and in a very short time we were settled in our new abode.

Our neighbours on either side turned out to be good, but not so fit as us, and as a goodwill gesture I dug both their gardens and mine at the same time, although I only planted my own. Every morning a social worker would be around the bungalows and if we needed her we just had to give her a wave. Sally and I soon realised that we had made the right decision and began to appreciate our surroundings. It was the next best thing to a country cottage — well, we were halfway into the countryside. We could catch the bus into town from the bus stop on the other side of the road and it stopped practically outside our house when it brought us home. And at the back of the bungalow there was a secluded square where we could park our car.

Jill and Ted came over for a visit and really liked the place. Jill had been working for Ansett Airlines for several years by now and they had been lucky enough to visit us practically every year, so the great distance didn't seem too bad. There were probably parents with children in other parts of the UK who saw their offspring less than we did.

Sally and I anticipated that we would both end our days in our delightful new surroundings — but that was not to be.

CHAPTER
TWENTY-SEVEN

Sour Gooseberries Revisited

Sally was waiting at the front door of our new home at Matson when I arrived back from the cattle market where I had gone to get some fresh eggs. We had only been there about a fortnight but already were beginning to make friends with the local people and congratulating ourselves on making the decision to take the place.

"I've just had a visitor — you'll never guess who it was," she said.

"Who was that, then?" I asked.

"Does the name Rosemary Jackson ring a bell?" she asked, smiling.

I thought for a moment. The name did seem familiar — then it all came back to me — the sour gooseberry caper!

"Of course I remember Rosemary Jackson," I said. "She was one of those three girls who pinched my gooseberries. What's she doing with herself these days, then?"

"You'll never guess in a hundred years," said Sally. "She said she wanted you to know that she has a lot to thank you for."

"I don't understand," I said.

"She said the lesson you taught her all those years ago paid off, and influenced her in her chosen career."

"What career's that, then?" I asked, completely puzzled.

"She's a PROBATION OFFICER," smiled Sally.

It was wonderful news.

CHAPTER
TWENTY-EIGHT

Emigration

Several years after moving to Matson, Sally had a stroke, and within twelve months she had died. The day it happened began like any other, with the early light creeping through the curtains to wake me. I was always the first to rise, since I didn't like lying in bed once awake, whereas Sally was quite happy to take advantage of a lie-in. There was a September nip in the air and I switched the heater on in the bedroom before going and filling the kettle in the kitchen. Once the tea was made I brought a cup of it back into the bedroom and placed it on a small table by her side of the bed.

"Cup of tea, Sally," I said softly. She stirred slightly, opened her eyes to look at me and then she just slipped away.

Although I had tried to prepare myself for such a possible event after Sally first had the stroke — since death seems just around the corner for anyone after a certain age, without any additional illnesses to speed its approach — nothing helped when it actually happened and coping with the loss seemed almost impossible to bear. We had been soul mates for so long.

When I phoned Jill in Australia to tell her the bad news, she booked herself on the first available flight home and was with me within 48 hours. She had already been home earlier in the year when Sally first had her stroke and had only returned home when things were improving and her mother was due for release from hospital.

After the funeral had taken place Jill and I talked about the future. She said that Ted and her wanted me to go and live with them — but I wasn't so sure. I was about 80 years of age at the time and didn't think it was a good time to emigrate. As Sally always used to say, I was too much of a John Bull at the best of times. To take on a new country at that age might be expecting too much, especially since it hadn't really appealed to me on my first trip. It was too hot and dry for my liking. Could I learn to like a place like that, I wondered?

Over the following weeks Jill addressed the situation several times. She had left the airlines by now to concentrate on her painting and in so doing would not be able to travel backwards and forwards to the UK as she had often done in the past.

"The point is, Dad," she said, "don't take too long deciding what you want to do, because the longer you take, the less chance you'll have of passing the necessary medical examination if you do decide to come."

A good point, I thought. I was a fit man for my age, albeit with a hip replacement, but who knows what's going to happen next year, next week or tomorrow? The

220

realities of losing Sally hit home in the everyday things of life, small things which I had taken for granted, like how we would sit together over breakfast, near the window in the lounge, assessing the skies as millions of other people in the country do naturally every morning, discussing what kind of day it was going to be, whether the rain would hold off whilst we went shopping or should we postpone our outing till the next day, and all the other daily chitchat which a person takes for granted. I would no longer have anyone to split the daily paper with like we had done all our married life, each of us having the piece we liked to read first, before swapping them over, later, and no more trips in the car.

After her stroke, we would sometimes drive up to Painswick Beacon or Birdlip with a flask of hot tea and park where there was a good view. No longer able to go for walks, we would sit and watch the distant clouds float across the sky and their corresponding shadows flow across the green fields below. And if the wind wasn't too strong we would wind the windows down to feel the fresh air on our faces so that when we returned home we felt as if we had walked in the open air — like we used to — even if we hadn't.

Eventually, after taking stock of my situation and realising that I would rather be with my family — even if it was a stinking hot place at the other end of the earth — than risk not seeing them again, I told Jill to go ahead and get my application to emigrate. She was overjoyed and the next day caught the train to London to start the ball rolling.

Six weeks later Jill returned to Australia. She would have stayed longer if I needed her, she said. Ted had told her to stay as long as necessary. But I reassured them that I would manage everything that end because Wally and his family had already offered their total support with any help if needed, and as my application progressed I became increasingly grateful for it. The whole thing didn't take long — perhaps things move faster when the person is old. In no time I was having my medical and the next thing the removers were packing my furniture for transportation, leaving me with just an electric kettle, a small fridge (which had already been spoken for), a few pieces of china, some cutlery, and a settee to sleep on for the last couple of weeks. I remember about a week later sitting on the settee in the empty room with Sally's ashes sitting on the floor beside me, thinking I had passed the point of no return — there was no going back. Even if I changed my mind at that point the chances were that the furniture was already on the high seas and there would have been chaos trying to get it all back. I thought about what would have happened if things had been different — if I had been the one to go first and Sally had been left. There would have been no doubt in her mind what decision to make. She loved Australia so much she would run all the way to Heathrow Airport to get on the first available flight.

"At least her final resting place will be in that country," I thought.

Then my airline tickets arrived and with Sally's ashes packed safely in my case I was on a plane bound for

222

Perth. On arrival my grandson met me at Perth Airport and he put me on a connecting flight north to my future home.

Perhaps it was the knowledge that Dampier was now my new home and there was no going back meant that the place slowly grew on me this time. Where I had previously only seen the harshness of the surrounding countryside, I now suddenly began to take note of the beauty of it all. Jill's paintings, no doubt, helped me to look and see the blues and mauves of the distant hills and the various shades of salmon pinks through to deep reds of the rocks and earth, depending on the time of day. By now she was regularly holding successful solo exhibitions of her paintings at the Walkington Theatre — a grand complex built at Karratha, a town now much expanded since our first visit, with a huge library and an adjoining extensive college providing tertiary education for students living in the North-West of Australia.

The ghost town of Cossack, which I had visited all those years before, now had many of its historical buildings restored. Also an all-weather road, above the high tide mark, ensured a safe journey to and from it whatever the tides. It also had an art gallery for local artists which was run by the caretaker, who was also a painter, and other local artists. I would go with Jill every Thursday to man it for the day. We would always try and get home before late afternoon though, otherwise we would be dodging the kangaroos for the whole journey. That was another thing I started taking

223

for granted — the 'roos. There was always a carcass on the road somewhere, sometimes fresh, other times not so fresh, like the ones you could smell from a hundred metres away before you even reached it. Even if you didn't smell it, the flocks of crows suddenly rising from the road in front of you would tell you all you needed to know.

Sometimes we travelled north to Port Hedland 350 kms away for various art competitions and exhibitions. On those occasions we would leave home in the early morning, unfortunately with the sun shining directly into our faces from the front and returning late afternoon with the sun again in our faces all the way back. Jill and Ted had a large air-conditioned van by then for such journeys and moving paintings about, so at least we travelled in comfort.

Port Hedland was a very dusty town, partly caused by the fact that the conveyor belt carrying the iron ore from the stockpiles to the ship loader ran along the main road; consequently when the winds blew in a certain direction the dust covered the town. However, the residents of the place loved their town.

"All the towns up here look as if they're as dead as doornails," Jill said one day. "But all you've got to do is scratch the surface and there's a hive of activities going on."

Most of the activities were to do with sporting clubs like Aussie Rules football, cricket, tennis, badminton, softball, and the Swimming Club at Karratha; that was besides a stock car racing circuit on the outskirts of Dampier. Then there was the Repertory, of course, for people more interested in the Arts. Jill had long since given up participating in the Repertory, although she never missed any of their productions.

"I couldn't manage both Repertory and painting," she said. "So painting won."

And instead of Ted making props for the Repertory, he was now making the frames for Jill's paintings.

Jill had also started writing more seriously. Over the years she had written short plays, various scenes for pantomimes and sketches for the music halls, but recently had completed a correspondence course on Creative Writing. The result of this was that she had formed the Dampier Writers' Group. There were only a couple of members, but they had enough enthusiasm for the whole town. Hamersley Iron was approached by the group for sponsorship and the company agreed to the printing of 500 copies of one of the group's stories every fortnight, providing it fitted on both sides of an A4 sheet of paper (and that one of the members carried out the work involved). After that it was just a matter of them collating it with the local Dampier Newsletter, which was also printed fortnightly. This was then inserted into the local newspaper and distributed to all the houses in the town by the local boy scouts.

So when I arrived it wasn't long before Jill gave me some pens and a pile of paper and told me to get cracking. So I did — and became their newest and oldest member.

I even managed to get a small vegetable patch going in the back garden — only for the few winter months, but we had some fresh tomatoes, lettuce and carrots for a while.

When it was time for Ted to retire and move to Perth, they were both very sad at the prospect, and strangely enough, so was I. After living in the place for that length of time, it had grown on me. Although I still missed the green grass of home — and always would — the North West had slowly and surely woven its magic spell. I found I liked the place and wanted to stay as well. Ted and Jill had lived in Dampier for 27 years and loved everything about it. He loved the work and she loved the scenery. As it was, Ted had been one of the lucky ones because he had been allowed to stay on at work much longer than the average worker, but in the end his time did arrive. Even then, though, the company was very good and let them stay in the house for another twelve months if they wished before leaving. Needless to say they accepted the offer.

Eventually the time came to move. They already owned a house in Perth, but the first couple of months in our new accommodation turned out to be most chaotic and depressing, even worse than when I was packing up to leave England. The problem was that the place was overcrowded with furniture. My grandson had been living there while he was at university and a couple of rooms had been let to other students; consequently the house was already full of furniture. So when we arrived with all our furniture from the North West, plus all my furniture, which had been waiting in storage, the whole house looked like an overflowing storage depot, with the large lounge stacked full with tea chests, piled three high. I remember thinking if ever there was a time when I wished for the quiet life — like the one I left behind in Matson — this was it.

It took about three months to sort it all out, but eventually everything seemed to fall into place. During the settling in period I turned my attention to the garden. It was large and I could see where two vegetable patches could be. At least the garden was big and in no time I had it dug up and vegetables growing.

We hadn't been in Perth very long when I bought two small burial sites, side by side at the Karrakatta Cemetery — one for Sally and one for me when my time comes. At last Sally was laid to rest in the land that she loved.

CHAPTER
TWENTY-NINE

Ada

We had been in Perth about six months when I had a phone call from Wally back home in Gloucester.

"Remember Ada Preece?" he asked.

The name rang a bell.

"You were mates with her brother," prompted Wally. "When you were young — Alf Preece."

"Oh, I can remember Alf all right," I said. "But I don't recollect having met his sister."

"Well, she was his younger sister and probably only a small kid at that time. She was a bit younger than me, which probably makes her about ten years younger than you. I knew her well — we all used to knock about together. Anyway, I was talking to one of her relations yesterday and they said that she emigrated to Australia with her family, quite a few years ago. I asked them whereabouts and they told me she's living in Western Australia, in a suburb of Perth called Gosnells. I don't know her address but you could probably find it in the telephone directory. Her married name's Ada Simms, although I understand that she's a widow now and has been for quite some time. They said she'd be thrilled to bits to talk to someone from Gloucester."

228

So would I, I thought, especially somebody from around Clapham. Emigrating to a new country when I was eighty years old hadn't been the best thing to do, but the alternative had been worse, and although it was good to be living with my family I really missed Gloucester and its way of life. To talk again to somebody from my background really appealed to me.

A quick check with Ted on the location of Gosnells revealed it was only about a half an hour's ride away. Jill found Ada's telephone number in the directory and I gave her a ring. Would she like to come over to our place for a cup of tea and a chat? I asked her. She willingly agreed and a couple of days later Ted picked her up and brought her home.

We had a lovely afternoon reminiscing and arrangements were made for Ted to take me to her house the following week. And so began a friendship which has continued ever since. Ada makes the pot of tea and I take the biscuits, happy to share a couple of hours of each other's company every week as we talk over events long past, Ada's large brown eyes lighting up and her small frame shaking with laughter as she recalls various events. No doubt we repeat the stories many times, but since our memories aren't getting any better we don't seem to notice. Sometimes Ada talks of her much-loved husband, Harry, and I talk about the love of my life, Sally, both agreeing how lucky we were to find our ideal partner.

We even travelled to England together one year, staying with our respective relations, but sharing various outings together. Both our families came to the airport to see us off. Since we couldn't walk any great distances without stopping for a rest, and would never have managed the endless walk from the aircraft to the arrivals lounge at Heathrow Airport, wheelchair assistance was arranged for us at both ends of the journey.

Besides her family, there were other friends of Ada's who came to see her off, making it into quite a splendid event. In their enthusiasm they had bought Ada a beautiful spray of flowers which they pinned to the lapel of her jacket, making her look as if she was closely connected to some marital event. When the time came for us to leave the departure lounge, two flight attendants arrived with our wheelchairs and we settled ourselves into them,

"Have a lovely holiday both of you," everybody shouted as they gathered round us with last minute kisses and hugs.

"Is it your honeymoon?" one of the attendants asked Ada, admiring the beautiful spray of flowers.

"Oh, no — we're just good friends!" replied Ada.

A look of surprised admiration swept across the attendant's face as she knowingly added two and two and made five.

Twice, we went for a week's holiday with Jill on a painting trip to Rottnest Island, which is a popular holiday destination situated not far offshore from Fremantle, and only a thirty-minute ferry ride away.

On one of my weekly visits Ada told me of her teenage years and how she became a local Clapham celebrity. I was surprised I hadn't heard about it before, since news like that usually travelled like wildfire, but soon realised that when it all happened I must have been already married to Sally and probably living in Birmingham.

All was revealed one winter's afternoon as we were sat around her glowing fire. I never seem to feel the cold like other people do. The heat in the summer is more of a problem for me. But that day it was slightly cooler and the room was cosily warm and inviting. Ada poured the tea and opened the biscuits.

"I used to work for Morelands," she said, handing me my cup.

"What, the match factory?" I asked.

"Yes," she said. "When I finished school at fourteen I spent a couple of months looking round for a job, which was a waste of time because there was no work about. I really wanted to get a job at Morelands Match Factory. All the girls in town wanted to get to Morelands because they were a good firm to work for. From what we 'eard, the conditions were good, and it was a lovely clean place. It 'ad everything going for it really. It seemed to me 'opeless because there were 'undreds queued up at Morelands gates every morning — all along Bristol Road and Clifton Road, standing three or four deep. I 'ad a problem though; I didn't want to stand in the queue. Per'aps it was because I was so young and felt embarrassed to be seen there, I don't know, but I dreaded the idea.

"At that time my Dad 'ad an allotment in Seabrook Road, near Denmark Road 'igh school, and 'e was quite friendly with the man who 'ad the allotment next to 'is.

Anyway, as luck would 'ave it, the man turned out to be a foreman at Morelands and when m'Dad told 'im 'ow much I wanted to work there, 'e said I was to go down to the factory the following Monday and stand in the queue and 'ave my name put down, like all the other girls.

"'Well, there you are,' Dad said afterwards, ''ere's yer chance, but you can't get around the queue 'owever 'ard you try.'

"With that, I did as 'e said and the following Monday joined all the other girls lined up along the pavement. The queue was already long by the time I arrived and it was ages before I reached the office. When we got there our names were put down in a big book by one of the two blokes working there. Afterwards we were sent off 'ome. I went back at dinner time, though, and queued into the afternoon and 'ad my name put down again, thinking that if I 'ad to queue, I might as well get my name down as often as possible. That way it might be noticed more, I thought. The next morning I turned up again and stood in the queue and 'adn't been there more than fifteen minutes when one of the men in the office walked along calling out my name. I had a job! It was my lucky day and I knew it was all down to the man on the next allotment to Dad, but I never breathed a word about it to any of the other girls I worked with.

"The 'ours were 7.30a.m. till 5p.m. I started in the Mill running out the veneer, doing the same job that your Lil was doing. We were good friends, Lil and me, and we 'ad a lovely time working together. It must 'ave been at least six months later when Mr. Pritchard, the

Works Manager, came along one morning and asked me if I would like to work in the new VPO room which was being opened upstairs. It sounded really grand and to 'ave actually been personally asked made me feel quite special and I immediately said I would. Afterwards the foreman of the veneer room came along and asked me what Mr. Pritchard wanted and I told 'im.

" 'What's going to 'appen if you don't like it?' 'e asked.

"I 'adn't thought of that and suddenly 'ad visions of me not liking the new job and not being able to go back to my old one, and what would our Mam do if I lost my job and I couldn't give 'er any more money to 'elp out. Things were really difficult at 'ome with not enough money to go round and my extra bit 'ad brought a smile to 'er face again, instead of looking worried all the time. So when I saw Mr. Pritchard a short time later I asked 'im about my position if those circumstances arose. 'e looked a bit surprised for a minute. Perhaps nobody 'ad ever asked 'im that question before. I wouldn't 'ave either, though, if the foreman 'adn't suggested it.

" 'I don't know the answer to that, Miss Preece,' 'e said after considering the question for a moment. 'I'll 'ave to find out for you.'

"Anyway, a couple of days later 'e told me it would be perfectly all right to return to my old job if I didn't like the new one. So I relaxed. My new job turned out to be lovely and the pay was good too. I got two pound thirty odd shillings a week with a two pound a month

233

bonus on the top, which I never got with the other job. I 'ad to do a quick check that everything was correct with the boxes of matches as they passed by in front of me, and was officially known as a 'Passer'.

"Mr. Moreland, the big boss, would sometimes walk through while we were working. When that 'appened, everybody would stop talking and really concentrated on their work. They all knew when 'e was about because from the moment he stepped inside the production room, a whisper 'the old man' would swiftly pass from one girl to the next through the couple of hundreds girls working there. He was a big stern looking man who was getting on a bit. Always perfectly dressed with a beautiful black bowler hat. Whether 'e 'ad any 'air underneath I never knew, because I never, ever, saw 'im without it. All the girls were scared to death of 'im — me included. We didn't want to do anything wrong while 'e was around and lose our jobs. It 'ad 'appened to others who didn't work properly.

"Well, I'd been working in the new job for over twelve months and loving every minute of it, when one morning the 'old man' whisper swept through the air. I carried on working steadily when I became aware that 'e 'adn't passed by. 'e'd stopped by the side of me, a couple of paces away. I didn't actually turn and look at 'im but I felt 'is presence and felt sick. All the girls around me were giving quick glances at what was going on. What 'ad I done wrong, I wondered. My mind raced through everything I could think of but as far as I could tell I'd done everything right. What would our

234

Mam do if I lost my job, I thought. With Dad out of work we'd never manage.

"Mr. Moreland must 'ave stood there for ten minutes but it felt more like 'alf an 'our. Eventually 'e moved away leaving me wondering what it 'ad all been about. I 'adn't seen 'im do that to any other girl. Sometimes 'e might 'ave paused 'ere and there if 'e wanted to check on something, but nothing like that. After 'e left I turned to Beat Smith, who worked next to me on the other side, and asked 'er if she knew what all that had been about.

"'I dunno,' she said. ''e 'ad a watch in 'is 'and, and at first I thought 'e was timing you but then I realised 'e was just watching you.'

"'Watching me?' I gasped. 'What for?'

"'I dunno,' said Beat, completely bewildered.

"'There must be something wrong with me — my clothes — something. Can you see anything?' I turned round quickly so she could give me a quick once over.

"'There's nothing wrong with you — 'onestly.'

"I'd 'ave been surprised if there 'ad been, because I made sure my clothes were clean every day I went to work. Then everybody around me said that I must 'ave done something wrong to get so much attention, and considering everything that 'ad 'appened it sounded like they were right.

"Next thing Mr. Pritchard came up to me and said: 'Miss Preece, the Governor would like to see you. 'e's waiting for you in the Mess Room, upstairs.'

"I nearly died, and when I walked down that room to the end of it, I felt like I was going to my execution, and judging from the look on all the other faces they thought the same thing too.

"'Don't worry, dear,' said Mr. Pritchard, as 'e accompanied me upstairs. ''is bark's worse than 'is bite.'

"When we reached the Mess Room, we found Mr. Moreland seated behind a table at one end of it. On a table in front of 'im was a neat pile of clothes.

"'Hello, Miss Preece,' 'e said, in a friendly manner. 'Would you be good enough to go into the next room and put these on for me?' Mr. Pritchard gave an encouraging nod and the clothes were passed across the table to me.

"It was all a bit bewildering and strange. What did 'trying on clothes' 'ave to do with making matches, I wondered? But I did as I was told, not wanting to lose my job. I soon discovered that the clothes were more like a fancy dress costume with beautiful leather riding boots, jodhpurs, a silk waistcoat with a Union Jack emblazoned on it across the front, a white silk tie, a frock coat, and a beautiful black top hat. Could 'e 'ave been sizing me up for it when 'e'd stopped and watched me earlier, I wondered? If so 'e 'ad a good eye because if fitted me perfectly.

"I tentatively walked back into the room and Mr. Moreland asked me to walk round in a circle in front of 'im and then back the other way. 'e seemed to be quite pleased with what 'e saw.

"'That's good. Thank you, Miss Preece,' 'e said. 'Now you can go and change back into your own clothes and return to work.'

"What a relief, I thought. Of course, all the other girls wanted to know what 'appened. Some said they thought they wouldn't be seeing me again after being called to see Mr. Moreland, like I was. It was usually a one-way passage. Then when I told them about the clothes it was treated with suspicion.

" 'What did 'e make you do that for?' one girl asked.

" 'I don't know, 'e didn't say,' I said.

" 'Don't make sense,' said another. 'I could understand it if we made clothes 'ere, but we don't.'

"By the time I returned 'ome that night, I'd begun to worry about the whole episode. I told our Mam about it, what the clothes consisted of, and 'ow I'd been asked to change into them. She said it sounded like a fancy dress or something.

" 'Per'aps 'e'd bought it for someone else,' she said, 'and wanted to see what it looked like before 'e gave it to them. Anyway, Ada, you didn't do anything wrong so you've got nothing to worry about.'

"All was revealed about five days later when a letter arrived addressed to my mother, informing 'er that I'd been chosen to be a 'Carnival Girl' and would represent Morelands Matches. I would travel the country and have all hotel expenses paid. My wages would be paid as usual plus an extra five pounds in my pocket. FIVE POUNDS — when we only had thirty shillings a week if you were on the dole and a man had to keep his family on that, it was a fortune. You imagine me going home with nearly seven pound a week — our mother couldn't get over it. She was also informed that

237

I would be chaperoned for the whole of my time away from home.

"Mr. Moreland chose four girls in the end — Molly Clarke, Beat Smith, Violet Parmison and me. I represented John Bull Matches. Molly was dressed in a red, white and blue dress and represented English Glory. Beat was dressed in black and yellow and represented Safety Matches, and Violet was dressed as a sailor and represented Jack Tar matches.

"We went to Carnival Balls all through the winter and always entered the Fancy Dress competitions. It was very exciting. One of the first ones we went to was in Wolverhampton or Birmingham — I can't remember which, but it was a really posh do. We all 'ad to march round so that everybody could see us. A man got first prize and 'e led us. 'e wore a sheet over 'im and empty bottles of spirits were 'anging off 'im everywhere. 'e'd gone as 'Departed Spirits'. I got the second prize and was given five pounds.

"Our chaperone was named Miss 'ewitt, and she did 'er job very well. So well, in fact, that she never let us out of 'er sight for long. We never got a chance to put a foot wrong even if we wanted to. She was more like a stern 'eadmistress than anything else.

" 'Ada,' she said, as I walked off the ballroom floor with the prize money still in my hand. 'What are you going to do with all that money?'

" 'Share it,' I said, automatically.

" 'Good,' she said.

" ''ow, I wasn't sure. Should I divide the prize money up, or buy gifts for the other girls? In the end I decided to wait until we returned to Gloucester. When we arrived back 'ome at the end of the first week, we were all called to Mr. Moreland's office.

" 'Well done, girls,' 'e said. 'Now, first, Miss Preece. I hear you did very well in getting second prize in the fancy dress and won five pounds. That money is for you to keep yourself — it's your prize. You did a lot of good work in promoting Morelands Matches. In fact all of you did, and I will give an extra ten shillings to the four of you for all your good work.'

"After that we travelled far and wide as Ambassadors for Morelands, and always accompanied by our chaperone. We never 'ad a chance to meet any young men, even if we wanted. I remember once a couple of blokes got chatting to us and asked us if we would like to go for a drink and we agreed. To our surprise Miss 'ewitt never attempted to stop us as we left with them, but she must 'ave watched where we went because no sooner did we 'ave our glasses of lemonade in our 'ands — we never drank anything other than lemonade — than she marched straight in, and in front of everybody, said: 'What are you girls doing in 'ere? And I'm surprised at you, Miss Preece!'

" 'What for?' I said. 'I 'aven't done anything wrong.' But she just tutted a lot and escorted us back to our 'otel as if we were still school children.

"I used to give Mam all the money I earned and she would give me some back if I wanted to go out at the weekend. She was so proud, walking along the street to the shops, with 'er 'andbag over 'er arm with something in it for a change. And when I was due to go away on another tour, all the neighbours would know about it and come out and queue around our Mam's front door to see me off. They'd watch me come out, all dressed up in my John Bull outfit, and climb into the chauffeur driven limousine, which was always sent especially to pick me up. Then they'd all wave me goodbye with smiles all over their faces as if I was going to the other end of the earth instead of somewhere like Sheffield. And I'd wave back to them all through the back window. Mam standing in the middle of them all, virtually bursting with pride each time I left."

Ada's face glowed happily with the memories.

"Those were the days, eh, Ada?" I said.

"Yes," she said, smiling — her thoughts still far away.

I have now been in Perth twelve years and in Australia fourteen. Will I ever get used to the endless, cloudless, skies and summer heat? I don't think so. I miss the English countryside too much. I miss the clouds, the rain, the trees and all the rest of it that makes up the English landscape. Now I can only dream of the luscious fields of home, the rambling hedges with blackberries growing wild just asking to be picked, the babbling brooks with juicy long grass covering their banks, patches of stinging nettles here and there with dock leaves close by to cure the sting. Primroses, daffodils and bluebells in spring, and Cranham Woods, where Sally and I would walk when an occasional hot summer's day was a novelty and not a survival test.

I realise that for all the things I miss, since moving to Australia, there are many things I am thankful for —

240

the most important being that I have my family around me, for which I am eternally grateful.

The second most important thing is — the house is air-conditioned.

Three months ago my sister Lilian died after a long illness and a month ago my brother Wally also died. He, too, had been ill for some time.

Ada and I still meet once a week.

Postscript

Bill passed peacefully away on 1st April, 2005

Also available in ISIS Large Print:

Bothy to Big Ben

Ben Coutts

Ben Coutts has packed much more into his 80-plus years than most mortals. Before the war he worked as a ponyman in Perthshire and rural Sussex. Once he had joined up, his wartime experiences were hilarious and tragic by turns. He fought in Africa, was seriously wounded in Tobruk, torpedoed on his trip home in the Laconia, bombed, and when he had made it to the UK, began a long recovery after a series of painful operations. He went on to become a farm-manager in the Highlands, a sheep farmer, a leading stock breeder, show judge and broadcaster, and even a would-be Westminster politician.

ISBN 0-7531-9304-3 (hb)
ISBN 0-7531-9305-1 (pb)

Enter Drum and Colours

Alan Brewin

The story of one young man's National service in the 1950s, and how he came to terms with two years' compulsory soldiering and the experiences he endured or enjoyed.

From basic infantry training in Yorkshire to his time spent in Libya and Malta, Alan Brewin details his personal experiences of Army life and the various people he met along the way.

ISBN 0-7531-9992-0 (hb)
ISBN 0-7531-9993-9 (pb)